The
Indie Writer's
Workshop

The Indie Writer's Workshop

Renda Belle Dodge

PINK FISH PRESS
SEATTLE, WASHINGTON

This book is for anyone who has ever picked up a pen and inspired me. Past, present and future.

In particular my mother, the first writer who showed me what it takes to be fearless. And my daughter, who recently started her first novel.

ISBN-13: 978-0615509624
ISBN-10: 0615509622

Book design © Pink Fish Press
Author photograph and Cover Photo © Renda Dodge
Edited by Tali Sherman-Hall

First published by Pink Fish Press 2011

Printed in the United States of America
First Edition

10 9 8 7 6 5 4 3 2 1

rendadodge.com
thepinkfishpress.com

PINK FISH PRESS
SEATTLE, WASHINGTON

Table of Contents

Introduction

The Emergence of the Independent Writer

Being a writer is easy. You sit down at your typer, you write words, you sell the words to a publisher and you roll around in piles of money. It's that easy, right? If you're reading this book, you have probably realized that it's not as easy as it might seem. We all have access to computers, paper & pen, and cellphones with keyboards and word processors. There's no stopping anyone who wants to write a book. This is amazing. It's also, to be honest, scary. There's a lot of crap out there and how are you, let alone the publishing companies, supposed to wade through it?

The major publishing companies, who I refer to as the "big six" (Hachette, HarperCollins, MacMillan, Penguin Group, Random House, Simon & Schuster—and all of their countless subsidiaries), are still working with the traditional methods of agents, submission and rejection, and subsequently only publish a fraction of the actual writing public.

With so many voices clamoring to be heard and traditional publishing companies stuck in the methods of last century, what are the options for a serious writer? There isn't a "wrong" way and a "right" way to publish your novel. I choose to share the benefits of independent publishing but that doesn't mean I'm on the right side of the issue. I'm obviously a proponent of indie publishing, but there is still value in the traditional methods. If you choose to go through traditional means there are one million and three books on how to do so (I suggest the Writer's Digest *Guide to Literary Agents*). However, if you find yourself as frustrated as I became with the hamster wheel of the commercial fiction market, you do have options. One of those is to take on the mantle of Indie Writer. For reference, Indie/Independent are the same thing, but I tend to use the term Indie on most occasions.

Indie publishing used to be called "self-publishing" and there's a lot of debate as to the actual difference, but in my opinion there isn't one. I started using the term Indie several years ago because I didn't like the stigma attached to individuals who chose to publish their own books. It's important to keep in mind that the stigma exists for a reason. We have all heard of, or met, someone who wrote a terrible book, with awful cover art and prose that lacked good editing. Usually these people also have thousands of copies of their own book taking up residence in their garage or attic. They can't give away a copy. Personally, I didn't want to be associated with the term. I've heard a million times (yes, I have a penchant for hyperbole) "That book *looks* self-published" and I didn't want people thinking that about my art.

Throughout this book, I'll share my triumphs and downfalls. There's a serious learning curve when it comes to creating your own small press. Oh yeah, by the way, that's what you'll be doing. It's probably time to start accepting the fact you're about to become an editor, a marketer, and a public speaker—among other things that will come up along the way. It took me a long time to accept these roles, but now I enjoy what I take from the challenges of the different tasks. I've been asked if independent publishing "works"; well, you're holding this book in your hands aren't you?

Accepting Your Art

All writers are artists. There I've said it; do you feel better now? I do. I've been pushing writers to accept themselves as artists for years. There's a lot of leeway given to the artistic mind, but writers push themselves into a creative corner. Instead of embracing the narrative and story they create, they push back and say things like "I'm just a writer." Nope, I'm sorry, you're wrong. You're not *just* a writer, you're an artist. You create worlds and people out thin air. You observe the world and reinterpret it through your own words. This is an amazing feat. Once you accept your writing as art, you are free to start looking at the whole publishing process through different eyes. Why would you want to craft and create a story, characters and narrative—only to hand your artistic baby over to someone else and kowtow to their desires for your work. If you were a painter instead of a writer, would you allow an editor to force you to change the color of mountain landscape? Why, then, would you allow them to rewrite a character that you've created? Your writing is not a product; it's a piece of art.

By choosing the indie writer's path, you are choosing to take control of your art from start to finish. And to be honest, it's the absolute best reason to make that choice.

When I changed my own perspective and accepted my writing as art, everything changed about the way I approached my craft. To be honest, this wasn't an overnight transition. A lot of my personal metamorphosis came through the publishing process, and I'll share many personal anecdotes in the pages of this book. I'm still asked by friends and colleagues if I'm "still looking" for an agent. The day eventually came that I could look anyone in the eye and say with all sincerity "No, I'm happy publishing my own art," and the best part is that it's true! I love producing my own books, the quarterly indie arts and writing journal *Line Zero* and publishing other phenomenal writers and artists through Pink Fish Press.

About the Book

The Indie Writer's Workshop is broken into four parts: Before Writing, While Writing, After Writing and Publishing. I've written the book assuming you already have an idea for your novel or have even started writing. The foundation of any good novel is the writing (grammar and mechanics) and storytelling. Starting with the basics of plot and structure will help you build a better narrative. The better your story and writing, the more readers will connect with it. If you write a good book, people will want to read it.

Think of this book as a journal for your artistic process. Doing the exercises and writing things down will help you take a story from idea, to draft, to complete published product. We're writers; it's what we do. I write in the margins of every book I own, fiction or not. When I read other books on writing, I found myself writing notes to myself about characters and plot points. This workbook provides a place for you to write your own thoughts. For those of you that don't like writing inside books, disregard the feeling, push it away and embrace the blanks waiting to be filled in. You'll get a lot more out of the book if you do. Still can't do it? You can always write your answers in a notebook or journal. The point is, get as much out of the experience as possible. It's meant to be an interactive adventure.

Personally, I have several copies of the workbook filled out with stories and ideas for different novels, including my published novel *Inked*. Originally, I wrote the "Before Writing" section as an accompaniment to the all-day plot workshops I run. There was such high demand for the information outside of the workshops that I created a basic spiral-bound version. With the inclusion of the information on publishing options, I figured it was time to publish an actual, accessible workbook.

After the writing process, I cover editing and revision, followed by a whirlwind tour of the publishing industry. When you complete the process you will be armed with a strong, well-written novel and confident in your options as you walk down your own path to publication.

Everyone has a story, isn't time you told yours?

Before Writing

"nothing can save

you

except

writing.

it keeps the walls

from

failing."

Charles Bukowski

Preparing to Write

Inspiration

Why do you write? It seems like a simple question, but it's quite hard to answer. Are you writing for fame, family, your children, entertainment, or just the sheer act of writing as creation? Where does that desire come from?

For me, it was inherent. My mother is a writer and my great-grandmother was a story teller. I was able to take the best of both and meld them together and form my passion for writing. I can't imagine a time without writing. I've heard of people who gave up writing after many rejections. To me that would be a sign to move on to another project or tactic, not give up writing entirely. Storytelling is in my blood. I write for my sanity. I write for the passion of it. Everyone writes for a reason. What's yours?

Passion. Merriam Webster defines passion as "intense, driving, or overmastering feeling or conviction." Writing should be something that drives you. It should be intense, like a love affair with your characters, story and art. Stop and think about the fire inside your chest. You know it's there. It started as a little spark, perhaps many years ago, but now you can feel it burning deep inside you. It's your story; it's your desire and passion waiting to come to life in the form of words, worlds and characters.

I've heard the statement "Someday, when I'm a writer I'll…" Guess what? The second you put your pen to paper (or, in this day and age, your fingers to keyboard) you became a writer. Take the title and own it. You're a writer and an artist. You're a creator of characters and worlds. Now, you just need to get those ideas out of your head and onto the page. Not writing is a writer's biggest downfall. It's time to get black on white.

why do you write?

I am a writer because: _____

_____

My motivation comes from: _____

_____

My inspirations are: _____

_____

My favorite writers are: _____

_____

My favorite books are: _____

_____

I want to write a novel because: _____

_____

Time Management for Writers

It would be exceptionally easy to make a living as a writer if all we had to do is sit back, let the inspiration flow and collect a check. In reality, our lives are crazy, hectic and rarely allow for creative pursuits. Kids have to get to school; pets have emergencies; cars break down; dishes, toilets and laundry have to be cleaned; and television and Internet can be really interesting and distracting. But if writing is truly a passion, it is your responsibility to make time for it.

I recently met a girl who, at 16 years old, has already completed three novels. How did she do it? She sets her alarm every day and writes for two hours in the morning before school. She has better writing habits than most people twice her age. I can't write in the mornings; I can only write fiction at night. I've learned this about myself and I plan my days to allow myself time to write at night.

I'm a full time writer and I'll be the first to admit that I have bad days. I get antsy if I spend a couple of days without writing, though, and I know I'm not the only one. Sometimes making time to write in a hectic schedule can improve your outlook, mood and quality of life.

On the next worksheet there are two grids. I've filled one out as an example, marking everything I could possibly have to do in a typical day. As you can see, there are blank spots. This is where writing fits. When completing your own time-grid, include everything you do in a week. If you complete your grid and notice a lack of blank, acquirable time, it's time to cut back on a few other things. Get a babysitter, ask your spouse to take your daughter to baseball practice, or record your favorite television show and watch it later as a reward. Don't forget when scheduling to include travel and prep times, you don't want to lose more writing time to adjust your schedule.

	Monday	Tuesday	Wednesday	Thursday	Friday	Saturday	Sunday
07:00 AM	Wake Up	Wake Up	Wake Up	Wake Up	Wake Up		
07:30 AM	Breakfast	Breakfast	Breakfast	Breakfast	Breakfast		
08:00 AM	Gym	Gym	Gym	Gym	Gym		
08:30 AM							
09:00 AM							
09:30 AM							
10:00 AM	Food/Rest	Food/Rest	Food/Rest	Food/Rest	Food/Rest		
10:30 AM	Hygiene	Hygiene	Hygiene	Hygiene	Hygiene		
11:00 AM							
11:30 AM	Work	Work	Work	Work	Work		
12:00 PM							
12:30 PM							
01:00 PM							
01:30 PM							
02:00 PM							
02:30 PM							
03:00 PM							
03:30 PM	Food/Family	Food/Family	Food/Family	Food/Family	Food/Family		
04:00 PM							
04:30 PM	Journaling	Journaling	Journaling	Journaling	Journaling		
05:00 PM	Writing	Writing	Writing	Writing	Writing		
05:30 PM							
06:00 PM							
06:30 PM							
07:00 PM							
07:30 PM							
08:00 PM							
08:30 PM	Work	Work	Work	Work	Work		
09:00 PM							
09:30 PM	Television	Television	Television	Television	Television		
10:00 PM							
10:30 PM	Reading	Reading	Reading	Reading	Reading		
11:00 PM							
11:30 PM	Sleep	Sleep	Sleep	Sleep	Sleep		

Sample Weekly Schedule

	Monday	Tuesday	Wednesday	Thursday	Friday	Saturday	Sunday

Your Weekly Schedule

Making Writing Time Productive

Now that you have time set aside for writing, make sure your time is fruitful. We can be our own worst enemies when it comes to productivity. Social networking and blogging can quickly replace the tasks you should be completing with your writing time. I'm going to be brutally honest here. You don't need to build your platform as a writer if your novel isn't done, revised and edited. You won't get as much benefit from Tweets or your blog if you don't have a book to show for your writing. These are great tools for you—once your novel is finished and ready to be read by all those followers.

I absolutely love my home office. I have a pink Betta fish named Plath, an orchid I've managed not to kill, piles of books, manuscripts, to-do lists, art and stuffed animals. I get a lot of work done in my office, but I get a lot of *writing* done at a coffee shop. It's important to realize when a space isn't productive. If every day you sit down in your home office and the kids are screaming in the room next to you, your neighbor is bothering you or you plain old just can't concentrate, reevaluate your writing space and time.

One of the reasons I love writing at my local, independent coffee shop is the lack of distractions (when you start thinking like an indie writer, you begin to recognize how you can help the independent entrepreneurs around you). The man who runs the coffee bar at Caffè Felice is not going to run up and ask me to make him lunch, read his email, edit his article or tie his shoe. (If he did, it might be somewhat creepy.) This is a great environment for me, and you have to find the space that works for you. Local coffee shops, writing establishments (here in Seattle we have the Richard Hugo House) or libraries. If you have the ability or time, creating a writing space at home works for some people as well. There's a lot more self-discipline that goes into writing at home (at least for me), but it may be the perfect space for you. Do what works.

Sometimes a change of pace is in order as well. I've found, particularly when I have deadlines, that even a blank wall can be distracting. A change in scenery can bring your writing back into focus. The goal is to find what works for you and continue to do it.

I listen to music while writing. Music helps block out distractions, and particular playlists, albums or artists get me in the right state of mind. Be careful not to choose music that will distract you, though. This entire book has been written to the music of Poe, Amanda Palmer, The xx, Alanis Morrisette, Tegan & Sara and The Material on random. It's all female vocalists and I've heard the songs a million times, so I'm never distracted by them. At one point someone suggested another female vocalist, but after I added her to the mix I found myself distracted every time she came on. I removed her immediately.

Let's face it, as much as we love writing, it can be a real pain in the ass some days. It takes a lot of energy and time to write a book, and the results aren't always great. I wrote four novels before writing the first book I was happy with—*Inked*. Along the way, I learned things about my own writing style, pacing, narrative and story structure, and I can't stress enough how important the act of writing is. Think of it as physical exercise. When you go to gym for the first time, or after a six month (or six year) break, you want to die after the first twenty to thirty minutes on the treadmill or elliptical. However, after several weeks you can go for forty-five minutes to an hour without any fatigue. Writing is exactly the same way. They (yes, the ominous "they") say it takes six weeks to establish a habit, good or bad. So start building good writing habits now. Once you form your habits, the actual act of writing will become easier.

———

Habits that have worked in the past: _____

_____

Music that works for me: _____

_____

Things that do not work for me: _____

_____

I'd like to try: _____

_____

The most productive writing spot has been: _____

_____

Creating Achievable Goals

Goals are so very important. They help you create milestones and recognize triumphs. They can also let you know when you're getting behind. I create self-imposed goals all the time, and I live within my own deadlines. By setting a time frame, I know when to push and when to take breaks. Goals can also help you surprise yourself—when you realize that you're several days ahead of schedule, or if you fall behind but are able to catch up.

When embarking on a first draft, you should have an idea of an end word count, an end chapter count or something tangible you can track. It's up to you what kind of goal you're going to make for yourself. Personally, I use one of two methods—either word count or bullet points on an outline.

Word Count—this one is pretty self-explanatory. I choose a daily, weekly or monthly goal. If I miss a day, I make it up the next day. It's a great way to build discipline. It's also great practice for more journalistic writing where you are allotted a certain word count. When you use word count as a goal, you learn to get your point across in the space you have. It's very cut and dried: have you made your words for the day? If not, it's time to pause *American Idol* and meet your goal.

National Novel Writing Month (nanowrimo.org) is an extreme example of word count-focused writing. The goal is to write a 50,000 word novel in 30 days. It's a no-excuses opportunity to write. Some people take this month as a time to sit down and seriously write, and others use it as a social outing and entertainment. However structured, it can be a productive model to follow.

Outline—another option is to create an outline of your novel. Break the story into scenes or chapters, and then assign yourself a daily goal. I've found that this method works better with non-fiction, which lends itself to outlines. Writing fiction is an organic process for me and I'm often creating as I write. If you write like that, you'll often be way off from your original outline—making it a poor yardstick to measure your progress. On the other hand, if you're the kind of person who can create a detailed outline ahead of time and not deviate from it, this could be the method for you.

You've used the time grid to fit writing into your daily routine, but what if something keeps you from using the time you set aside to write? We all have excuses for why we can't write. Recognizing and letting go of these excuses is another critical step to creating a productive writing environment. We all have them. There are three kinds of excuse. There's the ones you can't control: sickness (for me, it's migraines) or emergencies. There are the irritating, but manageable kind: lack of time, broken computer, taking the kids to school, work or season finale of your favorite show. And then there's the online games, watering the orchids one more time and checking your email for the 100th time in one day.

Any of these things potentially stands in the way of you completing your novel, but each one can be overcome. Can't write in the mornings because you're busy getting the kids ready for school? Set aside time in the afternoon for yourself. Behind on your writing because you're sick? Give yourself an extra hour for the next three days after you recover. Overwhelmed with social engagements? Let your friends know that you're writing for the next two weeks, but you'd be happy to spend time with them when your draft is completed. Excuses may have become second nature, but you will be surprised how easy it is to do away with them.

Use this worksheet to identify the three biggest challenges you face and the ways in which you will overcome them.

My Goal is: _____

I will complete this goal by: _____

Three things that stand in the way of my goal are:

1. _____

2. _____

3. _____

I will overcome these obstacles by:

1. _____

2. _____

3. _____

Editing While Writing

It's Sunday morning and all your household chores are done. You sit down in front of your computer with a steaming cup of tea and prepare to write. Three hours later you emerge from your office, your hair a mess and three sentences written. Hours lost trying to perfect three sentences.

It is so easy to become stuck while writing. You become your own editor and nitpick everything you type, which can lead to frustration and ultimately quitting in the middle of a wonderful draft. This happens because you are your harshest critic. It's time to get over yourself. I'm not telling you to throw grammar and punctuation to the wind and hope for the best, but I am giving you permission to lighten up. It is far better to move on from a troubling sentence and continue to write. If you stop and agonize, you're losing the momentum by focusing on minutia. Take a deep breath and let go. Leave the distressing sentences or scene and move on to the next. There is another time and place to work on these things and it's called revision. Right now, you're focused on completing your first draft.

I do a bit of editing while I write, but when I realize that it's going to bog me down, I stop and move on. Sometimes I mark the draft to remind myself there's something I need to revise in the section, but I am also aware that I will find it in editing. You don't miss much in the editing process. My pages look like they were recovered from a war zone once I'm done with the red pen. (Actually, in the last couple of years I've switched to purple pen.)

Ernest Hemingway once said "The first draft of anything is shit." It's true! No one writes a perfect first draft and anyone who claims to is lying. When this happens to you from here on out, remember Hemingway and keep writing.

Someday Publication

I use the term "writing for someday publication" a lot. When a well-known author writes a book or an article they write with publication in mind. You should do the same. Take everything you write seriously. You might not have a publisher standing outside your door waiting to hand you a contract, but your writing shouldn't reflect it. It should be crisp, fresh prose prepared for "someday publication."

Get Your Ideas onto Paper

Writers have ideas and those ideas turn into stories. You stand behind a woman at the coffee counter and make up her back story. You drive down the freeway and seeds blossom into full-fledged ideas (and, if you're like me, you wish you could drive and take notes at the same time). You question concepts and follow your train of thought to fantastical worlds and situations.

This is where novels are born. Hold onto these concepts, write them down, however small, and come back to them later. There are even times when you can combine several of your ideas into one novel. Don't give up on any of the characters or plots that populate your mind.

I've provided a couple of pages for you to record your favorite ideas. In the end, you will have to choose which one you'd like to develop into a full novel, but for now jot down characters and plot twists.

> *"Your aunt is a very lucky woman Angelica. She has two lives. The life she is living and the book she is writing."*
> *The Hours* (film)

1. Interesting Character Backstory: _____

_____

_____

2. Interesting Character Backstory: _____

_____

_____

3. Interesting Character Backstory: _____

_____

_____

1. Story Concept: _____

_____

_____

2. Story Concept: _____

_____

_____

3. Story Concept: _____

_____

_____

4. Story Concept: _____

_____

_____

5. Story Concept: _____

_____

_____

Why Write This Story?

There are three types of writing; the well-written story, the well-told story, and the book that does both. Truman Capote (*In Cold Blood, Breakfast at Tiffany's*) can write some beautiful sentences, but his narratives often lack focus or good storytelling. Chuck Palahniuk (*Fight Club, Survivor*) writes an interesting story, but he's not someone I'd cite as a great writer. Michael Cunningham (*The Hours, A Home at the End of the World*) is an example of someone who does both. These are my own opinions, and it's your job as a writer, and therefore a reader, to find your personal heroes and develop your writing style.

As you work through this book, you'll start learning to implement both strong storytelling and good mechanics. Anyone can learn to put a sentence together in a grammatically correct way, but it's your job to weave a story through those sentences. Good writing and storytelling are not mutually exclusive; they should work together to dazzle your readers through word choice, structure and story twists.

Writers, like all artists, are storytellers. Some say that every story has already been told, but I don't believe it. Your Junior College English 101 teacher might disagree, but if I told you to write a story about two lovers from rival families you wouldn't write *Romeo and Juliet*. I know this because structure and storytelling are completely different things. Even if a story shares the same plot structure, the way the story is told makes a big difference.

With this in mind, let's analyze your favorite story idea.

My basic story idea: _____

_____

My favorite thing about my story idea: _____

_____

Why does *this* story have to be told? _____

_____

What makes your story different?

Is it something compelling that everyone would want to know about?

_____

Something dramatic or emotional that people can relate to?

_____

Something historical that will interest readers?

_____

Is it your character that drives your story? What makes your character stand out? Is it the setting? What is so special about the setting? Are you really passionate about this story, character or setting, and will your passion translate to the readers?

_____

_____

_____

I always advise writing what you're passionate about, not what seems most popular. Don't write a young adult horror novel just because you think it will sell, write it because you're really passionate about the project. Your story, genre and audience will be determined by your passion. But it helps to keep in mind that you're writing *to be read*. Keep this goal in mind as you struggle through hard days, tough scenes and dry patches. Someday someone will read your novel and they will like it.

When I published *Inked,* I had no idea if I'd sell a single copy, but after a few weeks of promotion I started selling copies to complete strangers. I'm not a billionaire, but I shared my novel with people who read it. I accomplished what I set out to do. That first stranger, and the many who have read it since, are my audience. I'll talk more about audience and marketing in the second section of this book, when you have a completed novel you're ready to sell.

Audience

Someday people are going to read your book. This is your audience, and thinking about your target audience as you're writing helps you build a cohesive story.

My grandmother wrote the story of her life shortly before she died. It was forty pages of 8x11 sheets copied at Kinkos and stapled together. Her audience was her family, the people who knew her and wanted to remember her. It was funny and sad, but most of all it was a keepsake. If she'd been writing her memoir to a wide audience she would have had to change the family jokes and explain the nick-names. If you are writing just for your family or yourself, that is great, however if you are writing for someday publication it's important to keep in mind who will be reading.

I'm writing for:

☐ Myself

☐ My Family

☐ Genre Readers

☐ Women

☐ Men

☐ General Audiences

☐ Children

☐ Young Adult

☐ Middle Grade

☐ My Dog

☐ Other: _____

Genre

Genre is defined as "a category of artistic, musical or literary composition characterized by a particular style, form or content." Most novels fall into a certain genre, and it's important to know yours because you'll know what the audience expects. For example, most romance novels won't spend fifty pages describing a murder. This is because people who read romance novels aren't there to read gore. If you are writing a romance novel that contains such things, you might want to consider a change in genre.

There are more genres than we need to discuss here, but the main ones are listed below. You will probably fall into one of these categories, or one of their many sub-genres. For instance, post-apocalyptic is a sub-genre of speculative fiction, which is often considered a sub-genre of science fiction.

The goal here is to find where you fit. Are you writing a murder mystery? Check out the thriller and mystery genres. You'll probably fall into one of the categories. Are you writing something with vampires? Depending on your target audience you're probably writing young adult or horror. Narrow your list of potential genres to a few and do a little research. It should be pretty easy to figure out.

Circle the genre you believe your novel falls into and do some research.

Adventure

Comic

Experimental fiction

Erotic

Historical

LGBT fiction

Memoir

Occupational fiction

Political

Religious fiction

Saga (Family Saga)

Science Fiction

Horror

Fantasy

Suspense

Western

Women's Fiction

Tragedy

Urban

Thriller

Romance

Your Favorite Books

When everything comes together and a story is told well, it becomes one of those books you're hooked on reading. One of the best pieces of advice I can give to writers is to keep reading—especially in your own genre. When you spend time with the books you love you will influence the way you write. So, what hooked you into the last novel you couldn't stop reading?

Analyzing what you love can help you understand the important reader/character dynamic.

One of my favorite books is: _____

Why I loved this book: _____

_____

Let's say you're standing in your favorite section of a bookstore.

What questions to you ask yourself as you pull a book from the shelf?

_____

What draws you into a book? _____

What makes you take it from shelf to the checkout? _____

_____

How can you bring these elements into your story? _____

_____

Engaging the Reader

If a narrative falls flat or lacks interest, most people will put the book down. That's because the writer failed to engage the reader. Readers ask a lot of questions, often subconsciously, about your story as they read. We humans are inquisitive by nature and we're often thinking ahead and considering how the main character will react to situations. I can usually figure out how a movie will end because I'm constantly analyzing the story structure. Even if I know how it's going to end, a good story will still keep me interested the whole time.

As you write your novel, it's your job to keep the reader interested through dynamic characters, compelling storytelling and engaging setting. You should be able to stop at any point during a scene or chapter and answer these questions: What's this story/scene about? Is anything happening? Why should I care? Why should I keep reading?

Can you answer these questions about your general plot right now before you've even started writing? It's your job as the writer to answer these questions through dynamic characters, compelling storytelling and engaging setting.

"What is this story about?"

This should be a one to two sentence description. Think of it like the logline of a movie. Don't worry if it's rough right now, just get the general idea down. Some examples:

- "An Iowa housewife, stuck in her routine, must choose between true romance and the needs of her family." (*Bridges of Madison County*)
- "An epic tale of a 1940s New York Mafia family and their struggle to protect their empire, as the leadership switches from the father to his youngest son." (*The Godfather*)

My story is about: _____

_____

"Is anything happening?"

What is the main problem, issue or plot point your character is dealing with? A story needs verbs to make it interesting. What happens to your character to keep him (and the reader) involved in the story?

- *Alice in Wonderland*: She's trying to get home and keeps running into trouble.
- *Titanic*: First they're falling in love, and then the Titanic is sinking.

The main "thing" that is happening in my novel is: _____

_____

"Why should I care/Why should I keep reading?"

What is relatable about your plot or characters? What makes your story grab the reader and not let them go?

- *Alice in Wonderland*: We care about Alice because she's a little girl. We want to make sure she makes it out of Wonderland alive. Also, the fantastical nature of the world around her makes us wonder what will happen next.
- *Titanic*: We care about Rose and Jack, each of the characters were fleshed out in the movie and we want to see them survive and be together.

Reader's should care because: _____

_____

The 10 Steps to Creating a Masterpiece

1. Plot—The Plan

What: You can write a 200-page novel about an eccentric character doing nothing in a beautiful room, but who will read it? Plot is the plan for your novel. It's what is happening to your interesting characters in their detailed settings. Eventually your character is going to stand up, answer the phone and discover his wife has been killed, or some other interesting plot point. You wouldn't build a building without some sort of plan, why would you rush into a novel without one? Plot is the blueprint for your story.

How: As someone who reads many manuscripts, I can tell when someone has thought out the plot points. Conversely, I can tell when someone has written by the seat of their pants. While there is something to be said for "seat of the pants" writing, you'd better have a damn good editor to bring some consistency to the story.

Creating and sticking to a plot throughout a novel will help you create a cohesive, easy-to-read story.

"Easy reading is damn hard writing."
Nathaniel Hawthorne

2. Story Pacing

What: If you've attended any fiction writing classes, you've heard of the information dump. This indicates a writer unsure of where to start their story. In my early short stories I was guilty of this. I would give all the backstory in the world, sharing childhood traits and favorite teachers before getting into a story about childbirth.

This tactic can be used effectively sometimes, but you'll often lose the reader before you get to your point. While the detailed backstory may be important to the overall story, it's about how you present these facts.

How: Pacing starts with the beginning of your narrative, but consistency makes an amazing novel. Think about the important bits of your story, the absolute necessities, and then compare them to the detailed fluff that makes your character grow from an idea of a person into a real person. As you write, watch for uniformity in the way you present these facts.

If the character reminiscences about a day in high school at the beginning of every chapter, make sure you keep this consistent throughout the novel, unless there's a good reason to skip it. Keep the format and the tone the same each time you use this writing device. The same goes for other scenes or dialogue.

Remember, when the character isn't trying to achieve a goal, the plot is not happening. Keeping your story on track will help you pace your story.

"I try to leave out the parts that people skip."

Elmore Leonard

3. Themes and Ideas

What: Themes come from your plot. What are you trying to portray with your writing? Even a story about robot aliens taking over the planet through mind control has a theme. In the case of the robot aliens the theme could be "mankind will overcome" or the downfall of the human race. However you weave your story, there will be a theme in your writing.

How: Understanding your own themes and what you are trying to portray in your story is very important. It's easy to preach at your audience, though, and no one likes that in a novel. Go back and read your favorite novel, and watch how the author deftly inserts themes and ideas into the story. As you write, you should think about the plot, your blueprint, and stay on track. This will bring consistency to your writing (are you starting to see a theme in the ten steps yet?) and help your reader understand your intentions.

"The best style is the style you don't notice."

Somerset Maugham

4. Realistic and Believable Dialogue

What: Dialogue is the cornerstone of everyday conversations. You can't joke with the barista behind the counter, fight with your girlfriend or plan with your co-workers without it. It's one of the most natural things, but many writers can't write dialogue to save their manuscripts.

How: It's important to read your dialogue aloud, just to make sure it's realistic. Or better yet, have someone else read it aloud to you. This will help you listen for the bits that don't sound right. Another thing to keep in mind is extraneous speech. When Jen answers the phone, we don't need to read all her "yeah, uhms" and small talk unrelated to the story. Written dialogue is slightly different than normal speech; you want to get to the point of the conversation without including all of the extras we expect from speech.

"The role of a writer is not to say what we all can say, but what we are unable to say."

Anaïs Nin

5. Excellent Writing Mechanics

What: Writing well is the sign of someone who cares about their craft. Watch for consistent tone, tense, grammar and point of view to keep your reader in the story. Often in the first draft, these will be left to the wayside and (to a point) that's completely fine. I'm a terrible speller (thank goodness for spell check), and I learn new grammar rules every day.

How: Some writers go completely off the grammar train and free write their first drafts, while others labor over the mechanics while writing. This is a personal choice, but I've learned from months spent in revision hell that paying a bit of attention to the mechanics while writing will lead to easier revision. It's about finding balance between editing and writing. Don't allow grammar to be an excuse that keeps you from writing. Remember: Get black on white in the first draft, revise and perfect in the later stages.

Becoming a better writer isn't hard to do. Some authors seem to keep the secrets of their hold on the written word close to their heart, but it's really not a secret. It's practice and knowledge.

"I'm not a very good writer, but I'm an excellent rewriter."
James Michener

6. Intriguing Setting/Mood/Tone

What: You never want your story to be boring, so periodically review what you've written and make sure it has not grown stale. If you think you might be encroaching on the mundane, throw in a little spice and make it more interesting. Your characters and your readers will thank you.

How: Adding interest to your story through unique and interesting settings, events, mood and tone will make your reader turn the page faster and faster. If these aspects of your story are the same old thing they've read before, what's going to keep your reader engaged? Readers thrive on unique, so give it to them. Remember to stay realistic when creating unique though, as it still needs to believable and interesting.

"Fiction, imaginative work that is, is not dropped like a pebble upon the ground, as science may be; fiction is like a spider's web, attached ever so lightly perhaps, but still attached to life at all four corners."
Virginia Woolf

7. Haunting and Precise Description

What: The best writing is the kind that sticks with us or sends a shudder down our spines. A well-written story leaves you with memories of stimulating description. When a reader can smell the roses that bloom in the grandmother's garden or the squalor of a junk yard, you're doing your job right.

How: Avoid too many of adverbs (lovingly, precisely, slowly) and instead use more specific description to explain the scene. As your Creative Writing teacher probably told you, "show, don't tell." This concept seems to frustrate many writers; however all that it means is instead of saying "Bree was tired" you need to show us how tired she was. Describe her labored movements, yawns or her cranky attitude. Let us see the character's feelings and emotions with your description.

> *"Don't tell me the moon is shining; show me the glint of light on broken glass."*
> Anton Chekhov

8. Compelling and Human Characters

What: The characters you create are the reader's link to the story and the world you've created. No one wants the hero to be too perfect or the protagonist too flawed; we want realistic and human characters with interesting histories and traits.

How: Steal traits of the people around you and apply them to your characters. It can be fun! I often use someone I know as a template when I start writing a character, but as the characters develop they always become their own person.

> *"I am a man, and alive…For this reason I am a novelist. And being a novelist, I consider myself superior to the saint, the scientist, the philosopher, and the poet, who are all great masters of different bits of man alive, but never get the whole hog."*
> D.H. Lawrence

9. Creativity

What: There's a distinct difference between good writing and interesting, creative storytelling. I firmly believe that all writers are born with a sense of curiosity and wonder—and this leads to the creative aspects of novel-writing.

A few days ago I drove under an overpass, something I do several times per week, and I noticed the words "Emily is a bad girl" scrawled across the cement structure. I immediately started visualizing Emily's character and backstory. In the end, I decided she'd written the words herself in a moment of teenage angst.

This will not be my next novel, but it's an example of how a storyteller's brain works.

How: Having an interesting, unique story and realistic characters is the best way to create a memorable and compelling novel. Use your creativity to build upon the world as we understand it and then test the limits of our assumptions. Create amazing worlds and dynamic characters and your novel with stand on its own.

> *"Everything in life is writable about if you have the outgoing guts to do it, and the imagination to improvise. The worst enemy to creativity is self-doubt."*
> Sylvia Plath

10. Read, Read, Read

What: As I've mentioned several times in the course of this book, reading is a pivotal part of growing as a writer. It's like an apprenticeship with the masters. You can't sit down with Nabokov, but you can read everything that he's written. This goes for contemporary authors and artists as well. There's a craft to writing and it's not just innate talent—it's something you can learn. You have the collected works of countless skilled writers readily available.

How: Pick up books by popular authors in your genre. Once you have a feel for what is popular, read independent books in that genre. Find out what other writers around you are reading, and then read it too. Read completely outside your genre. Writing a horror novel? Read a mystery. Learn what defines other genres will help you understand yours.

10 Steps Checklist

My plot is: _____

_____

My themes and ideas are: _____

My unique setting and tone are: _____

The most creative thing about my idea is: _____

_____

I am currently reading: _____

My story follows logical pacing: YES _____ NO _____

My story has realistic and believable dialogue: YES _____ NO _____

My writing has excellent grammar and mechanics: YES _____ NO _____

I have haunting and well-written descriptions: YES _____ NO _____

I have compelling characters: YES _____ NO _____

Plot & Structure

Story Structure

The basic structure for any story is this: The main character attempts to reach a goal, meets with confrontation on the way and the conflict is eventually resolved. This pattern also repeats throughout each scene of the story.

Think about Alice. She goes to Wonderland and faces several confrontations on her journey through it. Her overarching goal is to get home but that conflicts with the struggle of traversing a strange place. In each scene she is confronted with a new obstacle. The scene's conflict is resolved when she overcomes that obstacle, and the process repeats until she finally gets home, resolving the larger conflict of the story.

The *Character* has a *Goal,* but is met with *Confrontation.*
They battle for a *Resolution.*

Keep this pacing in mind for scenes and chapters within your story too. As you reach a scene and ask yourself "What's next?" come back to this list, find where your story fits, and continue to the next logical progression.

Let's see this in action with Shakespeare's *Romeo and Juliet*.

Romeo (character) attends the Capulet gathering. He falls in love with Juliet and wants to marry her (goal), but learns that she is a Capulet, the sworn enemy of his family (confrontation). He urges her to marry him that day, to restore their family's unity (resolution).

That, of course, is only the first part of the story, but the cycle will continue until the end of the play.

You can do this with any story.

Frodo (character) finds himself in possession of the One Ring. He must protect the ring and return it to Rivendell (goal), however there are Ringwraiths, among others, who want the ring (confrontation). Frodo successfully (and with much help) makes it to Rivendell (resolution). Once there, Frodo (character) learns that the ring is more powerful than he thought, and he offers to carry the ring to Mordor and destroy it (goal). Sauron tries everything in his power to get the ring back (confrontations abound) and in the end the ring is destroyed (resolution).

The Plan

By this point you should have absolutely no problem filling out "The Plan" for your novel, so get to it! Leave blanks if you have to, but come back and fill them in later

I can't title things, but I'm great at naming. I usually refer to my novels by the main character's name for months, sometimes years. I still call *Inked,* my published novel, "Tori" occasionally. There was another time when someone asked me a question via email about my short story with the name of *Last Day of Summer*. I was confused for several hours until it dawned on me that she was asking about the story I thought of as *Bobby Stone*.

Character names have always been easy for me, but they can be extremely hard for other people. I use baby-name books and websites. When I meet someone with an interesting name, I take note for possible future use. Actually, that's how I named my daughter too. My friend Tali had a roommate in college and her name was Ciel. I loved the name (not the person in particular) and gave it to my daughter. I feel somewhat bad because my daughter has lived her entire young-adulthood explaining how to pronounce it (like the letters C and L), but then again I've spent my life explaining that I'm Renda, not Brenda.

Fill out this worksheet (in pencil if you need to). It will help you get through moments of writer's block. Plus, it will be great to look back when you've completed your novel and see if the actual final product lines up with your plan. If it doesn't, it's fine! It only means that you let the creative path lead you.

The Plan for my Novel

Title: _____

Main Character's Name: _____

My lead character is

    Male / Female

    Age: _____

    Nationality: _____

    Occupation: _____

    They love: _____

    They hate: _____

    Their best friend is: _____

    Married / Single / Still living at home

His/Her objective is _____

_____

She/He is confronted by _____ who oppose(s)

her/him because _____

The conflict will resolve when _____

Point of View

One of the important details to work out before you start writing is the point of view from which you plan to tell your story. This should stay consistent throughout the story, with few exceptions. Having a good grasp on the different perspectives will bring consistency to your storytelling. Just like everything that I'm sharing with you in this book, feel free to play with the rules, or break them, if it creates an intricate, interesting narrative.

First Person

"It was a queer, sultry summer, the summer they electrocuted the Rosenburgs, and I didn't know what I was doing in New York. I'm stupid about executions."
The Bell Jar, Sylvia Plath

The first-person POV is from one character's viewpoint—the narrator of the story. Only the feelings and observations from this character appear in the story. In first-person, the author can take advantage of the fact that the narrator may be unreliable, by either giving a skewed opinion of situations or deliberately misleading the reader.

One of the drawbacks of first-person POV is the inability to get inside the head of characters other than the narrator. This has to be achieved through dialogue and exposition, rather than telling. While this is not a bad thing, it can lead to complications for the writer. If you need to share the intimate thoughts of more than one character, first-person may not be the right choice for your story.

Second Person

"Today a man called from Long Beach. He left a long message on the answering machine, mumbling and shouting, talking fast and slow, swearing and threatening to call the police, to have you arrested."
Diary, Chuck Palahniuk

The second-person POV is similar to first-person because it's usually told from one character's perspective. However, instead of Bob talking to us about himself, it is Bob talking to us about ourselves. Sometimes the narration is directed at another character in the story (which is the case in *Diary),* but most often it's directed at the audience.

This POV can make the reader feel like they are in the story, but this is not used often because it is a very hard technique to manage. The jarring reference to "you" can often pull the reader out of your narrative, which is the last thing you want to do.

Third Person

"Alice was beginning to get very tired of sitting by her sister on the bank, and of having nothing to do: once or twice she had peeped into the book her sister was reading, but it had no pictures or conversations in it, 'and what is the use of a book,' thought Alice, 'without pictures or conversations?'"

Alice's Adventures in Wonderland, Lewis Carroll

The third-person POV is the most common and can be divided into several different sub-types.

Third Person Subjective: The third-person subjective is used when the narrator is not an involved character in the story. In this perspective the narrator may convey the thoughts, feelings and opinions of one or more characters.

Third Person Objective: The third-person objective narrator tells a story without detailing any characters' thoughts or feelings. This point of view records observable actions like a movie, but not the thoughts of the characters. The third-person objective is preferred in pieces that need to present a neutral or unbiased view of events.

Third Person Limited/Omniscient: If the story is seen through the mind of a single character it is third-person limited, because the audience is limited to the perspective of that character. The third-person omniscient perspective is told from the point of view of a narrator who knows everything about multiple characters. Third-person omniscient can also be universal omniscient, in which the narrator reveals information that the characters do not have.

Voice

Voice is a simple, but often hard to explain, concept in creative writing. When it comes down to it, voice is consistency (I know, I sound like a broken record). As you're writing, you should maintain the same tone, relative sentence structure and storytelling. If you're writing from a character's perspective, it's all about speaking in the same way the character would speak, reacting the way a character would react and not breaking that character throughout the story.

Plot Types

Below are some basic plots and themes that have existed since stories were invented around the camp fire. It's important to keep in mind that some of the best and most compelling novels have come into existence when the author, having a firm grip on their themes, plays with our expectations. Also, stories may fall into more than one category, which makes them more thought-provoking and relatable. Often the sub-plots, of which there can be many, are of very different types.

I use movies specifically in this section because they are a more accessible and easily watched. Even if you haven't seen *Forrest Gump*, you probably know the basic premise.

Quest/The Heroes Journey

The characters search for a person, place or thing of importance, and the quest changes the main character as a person. *Finding Nemo, Star Wars, Lord of the Rings, The Matrix, Harry Potter.*

Example: Marlin (character) searches for Nemo (person—well, a fish). Marlin changes as he befriends Dory and is eventually reunited with his son.

Adventure

The difference between Quest and Adventure is the focus. Adventure focuses on the journey rather than the character's development. *Jurassic Park, Pirates of the Caribbean, Indiana Jones.*

Example: *Jurassic Park* has main characters, but the focus is on the action, the dinosaurs and the escape. In the end, the characters haven't really changed.

Pursuit

One person pursues another person or thing that eludes them. Like Adventure, the focus is on the pursuit, not the characters. *The Terminator Series, The Fugitive, Twister.*

Example: There's a love sub-plot in Twister, but the main story is about chasing tornadoes.

Revenge

The main character, who usually has the moral upper hand, seeks revenge for some wrong doing. It is emotionally driven, and usually also violent. I had a hard time coming up with any family-friendly examples involving revenge, however most comic-book heroes are based on revenge. *Spiderman, Hamlet, Kill Bill.*

Example: Peter Parker is bitten by a radioactive spider, but he doesn't fully embrace becoming Spiderman until his uncle is killed.

Love

Something comes between two lovers, or potential lovers, and they must overcome it to be together. One of the characters will change drastically. *Titanic, Romeo and Juliet, Cinderella,* every romantic comedy.

Example: Rose and Jack are separated by class and her engagement, but they choose to be together anyway. They face another, larger, obstacle when the Titanic starts sinking.

Underdog

As the main character fights against the opposition, the odds are stacked high against him. *Forrest Gump, Karate Kid, Rocky, Mighty Ducks* (most sports movies), *Harry Potter.*

Example: Harry Potter is just an orphaned wizard, but he's the only one that can take on Voldemort.

One Against

The main character is fighting for the betterment of the community, but does not have their support. The lead's inspiration to the community often comes through self-sacrifice. *The Princess Bride, I am Legend* (Movie), *Avatar.*

Example: Sully is a disabled ex-marine (who is also an underdog), and he must go against his human community for the greater good of the Na'vi community. His self-sacrifice is that bond.

Allegory

Each character in the story represents an idea. The story as a whole is meant to demonstrate the consequences of those ideas. *Chronicles of Narnia, Pan's Labyrinth, Animal Farm*

Example: In *Pan's Labyrinth,* Ofelia represents the loss of innocence and immersion into the horrors of war.

Transformation

The character encounters a series of events that spur drastic change in the person's life. The change is most often resisted at first. *Bruce Almighty, A Christmas Carol, Metamorphosis.*

Example: Bruce is given all the powers of God and believes this will make him happy. In fact, he learns humility and selflessness.

My story falls into the _____ category because: _____

_____

Beginnings

The Hook

*"In another moment down went Alice after it, never once considering
how in the world she was to get out again."*
Lewis Carroll, *Alice's Adventures in Wonderland*

How do you pull your character and, subsequently, your readers, into your story? What is the "can't walk away from it" moment at the beginning? That's your hook; it's that simple. Something has to happen that your character can't abandon, escape, or neglect without dire consequences.

Once Alice goes down the rabbit hole, she's stuck. Carroll wrote her into dire circumstances within the first few paragraphs and didn't give her an out until the end. It's a simple but believable hook.

Remember, you want to avoid annoying the reader. Your reader could end up very frustrated (including, but not limited to, screaming and throwing your book) when your character, for no apparent reason, goes wandering into the abandoned lumber mill shortly after seeing the image of the drifter her boyfriend had killed earlier that night. Your story, your hook and your narrative need to make sense.

Alice's hook was the rabbit hole.

Frodo's was the impending end of the world.

The Three Act Structure

The three act structure works well because it's familiar—beginning, middle, end. It's closely tied to the ebb and flow of our own lives. We're born and live as children, we mature and live out our middle years and then we die. It sounds morbid, but it's true.

Act One	Act Two	Act Three
Set up the character's normal life and the change that will thrust them into act two. Establish the reader's connection to the main character.	The character faces their opposition, usually with a number of setbacks. The bulk of the story and the character arc are shown in act two. All of the action is leading to act three.	The character faces the opposition and resolves personal conflict.
The Hook Is Here. *Why can't the character walk away?*	*At the end of act two the character chooses to battle the opposition for the final time.*	*The story ends.*

Alice in Wonderland

Act One: Alice is reading with her sister and daydreaming when she is distracted by the White Rabbit. She follows him to his hole and enters Wonderland.

The Hook: Why can't she leave? Because she's literally stuck in Wonderland and must find her way out.

Act Two: Alice wanders around Wonderland and has a series of confrontations as she tries to get home.

Act Three: Alice faces the Queen's wrath and has to fight against her to escape.

—————————————

Lord of the Rings

Act One: Frodo enjoys his peaceful hobbit-life, but everything changes when Bilbo leaves the ring with him.

The Hook: Frodo is not hooked into the story just because he takes the ring, because he can walk away at any time. The hook is the danger the ring poses to the rest of the world. Frodo decides to take the ring to Mordor once he sees the evil it brings out in the rest of the group. If he ignores the ring, the world is doomed, and *this is the real hook*.

Act Two: Books and books worth of drama and character building (character, goal, conflict, resolution as we talked about earlier).

Act Three: Frodo chooses to go to Mordor alone and dispose of the ring. Even though Sam and Gollum tag along, it's Frodo's journey.

[As a side note on conflict/resolution, it's important to notice that Frodo never actually faces Sauron head on, but there's a constant character/goal/conflict/resolution cycle going on. It's a fascinating way of storytelling, and one of the reasons these books have remained so popular.]

Analyzing the Three Act Structure

Choose a favorite book or movie and analyze the plot's hook and structure.

Three Act Structure

Book or Movie: _____

What is the character's hook? _____

_____

Why can't they walk away? _____

_____

The first act begins: _____

_____

The second act begins when: _____

_____

The opposition is: _____

The third act resolves when: _____

_____

Now, do the same for your story.

My Three Acts

What is your character's hook? _____

_____

Why can't they walk away? _____

_____

My first act begins: _____

_____

My second act begins when: _____

_____

My third act resolves when: _____

_____

Where to Begin

Where to start your story can be one of the hardest parts of writing. Your character has lived their whole life in your created world and now suddenly you're going to come barging in.

In my opinion, it's best to start shortly before the hook. This will help keep the reader from becoming lost in a lot of backstory. Stop and think about where your story has to start in order to make sense to the reader, and then get them into the action with the hook as soon as possible.

It's also helpful and important that your character start the story in their normal, daily routine to orientate the reader. If your character is a kindergarten teacher living in Los Angeles, give your readers a glimpse of her life before the hook. Let her become a real human being that we care about. You want the reader to believe in the reality of the scenario. And then, once you've made us believe, hook her into the story.

The beginning of your story should: Hook the reader. Show the character's normal life and give the reader a sense of what's at stake. Create a bond between the readers and your character. Send the character through to the second act.

To Prologue or Not to Prologue?

I've heard some writers/agents/editors say any story that has a prologue or epilogue it wasn't started or ended in the proper place. I don't fully agree, but I understand the sentiment.

If your novel has a prologue, read it over again with a fresh perspective. Is the information that you've included something you can weave into the backstory later? If it's pivotal, reconsider where you've started the novel. Maybe you need to flesh out the prologue and make it your first chapter.

Some genres, such as fantasy or sci-fi, are far more forgiving of prologues. There are times when a prologue is needed to establish the world, government or alien race featured in your story.

First Sentences

Every writer wants to have the perfect first sentence, something that sticks with the reader and won't fall flat. Not every novel will have a "It was the best of times, it was the worst of times" first sentence, but you should spend some time with your favorite novels and look through their first lines for inspiration. This is something to labor over on your final draft, though. For now, write whatever fits and come back to it during revision.

Here are some examples of memorable first sentences:

"My wound is geography. It is also my anchorage, my port of call."
The Prince of Tides, Pat Conroy

"It is a truth universally acknowledged that a single man in possession of a good fortune must be in want of a wife."
Pride and Prejudice, Jane Austen

"It is a truth universally acknowledged that a zombie in possession of brains must be in want of more brains."
Pride and Prejudice and Zombies, Seth Grahame-Smith

"As Gregor Samsa awoke one morning from uneasy dreams he found himself transformed in his bed into a gigantic insect."
Metamorphosis, Franz Kafka

One of my favorite first sentences: _____

_____

Another one of my favorite first sentences: _____

_____

Typical Mistakes

Information Dump

If your reader has to wade through a huge amount of information before the hook, you may lose them. Once again, if you feel the entire backstory *must* appear at the beginning, you should reconsider where you are starting your story.

"And then, and then, and then–"

Starting your story with quick spurts of action, and little time spent on any one event, will disconnect your reader. Remember, the goal is to grab them and bond them to your story and characters.

Completely alienating the main character

Even if you're writing a story about a jaded ex-cop there has to be something in that first scene that shows the reader know he's human, something that makes us want to root for him. If the main character has no redeeming qualities, the reader will want to see the worst come to them, and you don't want that.

Long boring descriptions

There's nothing interesting about reading five pages of description of a house, only to have the character drive past it, never to return. Description related to the plot is good, but be wary of driving away the reader by making them ask, "What's the point?" and not giving them an answer.

Different Ways to Start a Scene

There are many strong ways to start a scene, whether it's the first scene of the book or any that follow. I'm going to let these four examples from published books speak for themselves.

Action

"If my father caught me he would cut my neck, so I just kept going. Broken sticks and sharp stones gouged my bare feet, but I didn't consider the sensation. A branch whipped across my face; I felt the sting and for an instant I was fully blind, but I didn't stop."

A Wolf at the Table, Augusten Burroughs

Raw Emotion

"CLARE: It's hard being left behind. I wait for Henry, not knowing where he is, wondering if he's okay. It's hard to be the one who stays.

I keep myself busy. Time goes faster that way.

I go to sleep alone, and wake up alone. I take walks. I work until I'm tired. I watch the wind play with the trash that's been under the snow all winter. Everything seems so simple until you think about it. Why is love intensified by absence?"

The Time Traveler's Wife, Audrey Niffennegger

Dialogue

"'Sir?' she repeats. 'How soon do you want it to get there?'

I rub two fingers, hard, over my left eyebrow. The throbbing has becoming intense. 'It doesn't matter,' I say.

The clerk takes the package. The same shoebox that sat on my porch less than twenty-four hours ago; rewrapped in a brown paper bag, sealed with clear packing tape, exactly as I had received it. But now addressed with a new name. The next name on Hannah Baker's list."

Thirteen Reasons Why, Jay Asher

Attitude

"Mr. and Mrs. Dursley, of number four Privet Drive, were proud to say that they were perfectly normal, thank you very much."

Harry Potter and the Sorcerer's Stone, J. K. Rowling

Middles

Unnecessary Bulk

No one wants to trudge through an uninteresting middle filled with extraneous details, boring side-steps and winding story lines that never seem to end. An excellent question to ask yourself when writing a scene is "What is this scene trying to accomplish?"

In other words, what is the meaning behind the scene, why is it happening and why should the reader care? I find this question so important I have it on a post-it note above my desk. If you can't identify the scene's purpose, maybe it's time to reevaluate the action happening in the sequence.

Anton Chekhov said: "If you say in the first chapter that there is a rifle hanging on the wall, in the second or third chapter it absolutely must go off. If it's not going to be fired, it shouldn't be hanging there." Ask yourself as you're writing, "Why am I writing this?" and make sure it's a question you can answer, for your readers and your characters.

When you're trying to achieve daily, weekly or monthly word count goals, it's easy to start rambling. That's OK. Make your word count and ask these questions when you come back to revise the draft. There's no rule that your first draft has to be gold, and if you are remembering the Hemingway quote, you know it won't be. You're going to end up revising it several times anyway. So go ahead, describe that turtle for four pages, but just know when it comes time to revise you'll want to ask yourself again, "What's the scene question? Why is this here? How important is that turtle?"

Avoiding a Sluggish Middle

The middle is where the majority of your story will be told. Your character will fight the opposition while encountering personal battles that will seem destined to keep him from achieving victory. Without good flow and a lot of entertaining events going on, your middle may fall flat.

Keep reminding yourself of : Character, Goal, Confrontation, Resolution.

This will keep your story flowing forward. Remember, if your character is not doing something, there is no plot. The second act, or middle, of your story should contain a series of events for your character, and they should all relate to the main conflict of the story. The middle is also an excellent place to introduce new characters and subplots.

Subplots

A subplot is a series of events that create a mini-story within the main plot of the novel. This can be a romance between two characters, a section that focuses on supporting characters, or backstory told through flashbacks. The subplot should always somehow relate back to the overarching story.

Often when introducing subplots you introducing new characters as well. Follow the same guidelines we've already discussed. Be sure to avoid information dumps, and make sure you connect the reader to your secondary characters as much as you have with the main character.

Examples:
—Marlin and Dory's friendship in *Finding Nemo*.
—The Titanic sinking is actually a subplot to the love story.
—Merry and Pippin's journey in *Lord of The Rings*. (Their story is one of many subplots in the books, Arwen and Strider's romance is another.)
—Han and Leia's romance in *Star Wars*.

My subplots are: _____

_____

I introduce these characters in my subplots: _____

_____

Raising the Stakes

The middle of your story is the reader's chance to get to know the character better and develop a deeper connection with them. An excellent way to do this is by raising the stakes for the character. It is far more believable for things to get worse than better, and this works because we humans identify with and care about someone in jeopardy. We may resent somebody who wins the lottery and finds their long lost father, all on one day; but you feel sorry for the guy who loses his girlfriend, gets in a car wreck and spills coffee on himself. Haven't we all had days like that?

What follows is an excellent example of why I shouldn't write thrillers, but bear with me.

Personal Stakes

Example: As Dylan ducks into an alley, he receives a text message from his girlfriend, Ashley, breaking off their relationship.

How can things get more emotionally detrimental for my character?

_____

_____

Example: As Dylan ducks into an alley he receives a call from the "bad guy." His girlfriend has been taken hostage until he returns the goods he stole.

Is there someone my character cares about who can get caught up in the action?

_____

_____

Example: Dylan has been stealing from his boss to conceal his father's sordid past with the mob.

Are there dark secrets from the past that can be revealed?

_____

_____

Culture Stakes:

    Example: Dylan's father is a senator who is about to pass a major environmental bill.

    What social aspects are affected by the story?

_____

_____

    Example: Dylan's father's bill is controversial and many people oppose its implementation.

    Are your characters with some huge issue?

_____

_____

Story Stakes:

    Example: While running from the cops, Dylan shatters his ankle.

    What physical harm can come to my character?

_____

_____

    Example: Dylan's best friend from college is the son of the mob boss.

    What characters can I introduce that will make things worse for my character?

_____

_____

These are just a few of the many ways you can put more at stake.
Keep asking: "Can it get worse, but still be believable?"

Endings

Types of Endings

The ending should wrap up loose ends, complete the story and finish your character's journey. There is nothing more frustrating to a reader than a story that leaves things hanging. The end should reflect the tone of your story and adequately portray your character's response. If you can't end your story well, what was the reason to tell it?

Positive Ending

Everything works out for the main characters. Almost all comedies and underdog stories will end with a happy conclusion.

Examples: *Seabiscuit, Pretty Woman, Knocked Up, The Waterboy, Cinderella*

Ambiguous Ending

Everything might have worked out well for the characters, but we're not sure. It's left up to our imagination, or it may be the result of vague storytelling. Horror movies love to use ambiguous endings.

Examples: *Inception, Memento, LOST, The Grudge*

Negative Ending

It's a tragedy, and we all love a tragedy because it's human nature in action. These stories tend to be high drama, and often end with death.

Examples: *The Virgin Suicides, Romeo and Juliet, Revolutionary Road, Into the Wild*

Positive Ending for the Character, but bad overall

The main character is better off, but most of the world isn't. Whatever danger posed a threat (and often the danger *is* the main character) is still out there, and usually it's still mad.

Examples: *Fight Club, Memento, Kill Bill*

Negative Ending for the Character, but good overall

The character may not have gotten what they wanted, or they ended up dead, but they helped a group of people in the process.

Examples: *I am Legend, The Matrix*

The best stories end with:

I enjoy ending that are: ☐ Marriage/Romance

☐ Happy ☐ Death My novel needs a

☐ Sad ☐ Justice ☐ Positive

☐ Dramatic ☐ Rebuilding ☐ Negative

☐ Confusing ☐ Reconciliation ☐ Ambiguous

☐ Tragic ☐ Starting over ☐ Complex ending

☐ Romantic endings ☐ Explosions

10 Possible Endings

Do you know how your book is going to end? Sometimes writers end up locked in a creative standoff with themselves, and you may not even realize that you've been holding out on your own creative process. Whether or not you know how your book is going to end, write down ten possible endings for your story—no matter how absurd. There might be a seed of an idea in there.

If you know your ending, this exercise may help you expand your ideas and build into your current plan.

1. _____

_____

2. _____

_____

3. _____

_____

4. _____

_____

5. _____

6. _____

_____

7. _____

_____

8. _____

_____

9. _____

_____

10. _____

_____

Characters

The Character Arc

In any story, the reader is connected to the action by the main character. Throughout the novel, the reader is drawn into what the lead is thinking, feeling and experiencing. A major element is the arc of the character's development over time. The foundation of your story is the character's experience of the plot, so the character arc is tied closely to it.

Typical Character Arc:

- Meet the character
- Introduce his beliefs and personal morality
- The character is hooked into the story
- Conflicts inside the narrative impact the characters beliefs
- The character's beliefs are challenged; he must stand up for himself
- The character experiences an epiphany, a moment of significant change
- Resolution

Alice's Character Arc:

- We meet Alice and she seems disinterested and bored with her childhood. She is very precocious and acts without thinking of consequences.
- Alice is hooked into the story by following the White Rabbit down his hole. At first she is taken in by its magical and exotic landscape.
- Several incidents happen that frustrate and impede Alice's ability to navigate Wonderland. She starts to see the consequences of her actions.
- The final straw comes from the Queen's rudeness and death sentence.
- Alice realizes she no longer wants to be in Wonderland and fights back against the Queen and the Card Guards.
- Alice returns home (wakes up) with new perspective. She's grown up.

Building Character Arcs

Pick a favorite character from a movie or book and fill out the arc below for that character. Keep the character's whole story in mind.

Favorite Character Arc:

The character : _____

Starts the story in his normal life by:_____

S/he is hooked by: _____

These incidents test the character:

1. _____

2. _____

3. _____

The character's beliefs are: _____

These beliefs are challenged when: _____

The character values these things: _____

These values are tested when: _____

The character's outlook on life is:_____

This outlook is shattered when: _____

The character's strong opinions are: _____

These opinions are threatened when: _____

Their epiphany moment: _____

The aftermath is: _____

Building Character Arcs

Now, do the same for your own character.

My Character Arc:

My character : _____

Starts the story in his normal life by:_____

S/he is hooked by: _____

These incidents test my character:

1. _____

2. _____

3. _____

My character's beliefs are: _____

These beliefs will be challenged when: _____

My character values these things: _____

These values will be tested when: _____

My character's outlook on life is:_____

This outlook will be shattered when: _____

My character's strong opinions are: _____

These opinions are threatened when: _____

Their epiphany moment: _____

The aftermath is: _____

Creating Character Bonds

It's often argued that the difference between literary fiction and commercial fiction is the focus. Literary is supposedly character-based, while commercial is plot-based. I disagree. All stories are told through characters and based on their experience of the plot. Nothing and no one in your story is as important as your main character. He or she bonds the reader to your novel through their actions and emotions, and if your reader doesn't feel that bond your story may fall flat.

When you meet someone new and realize you don't like them very much, what drives you away? Usually it's a lack of common ground or basic understanding. The same will happen if your readers can't relate to your main character. It's your job as a writer to create that bond with the reader and make it stick. Even unpleasant characters can be likeable; it's about the presentation.

Common types of character bonds:

Identification

Neo from *The Matrix*. Jack from *Titanic*. We get it because we go to work every day, pay bills, have children and make pot roast too. He goes to work every day. She hates her boss. He's the everyman. You can see yourself in these characters.

Sympathy

Jake Sully from *Avatar*. Cinderella. Harry Potter. They are orphaned, disabled, alone and we feel sorry for them. They've been given an unfair start and we want to see them triumph.

Jeopardy

Nemo in *Finding Nemo*. Harry Potter, again. We feel the danger. Nemo is out in the ocean all alone and he's just a kid. Harry Potter is sought after by Voldemort and we want him to get away. It's the sense that we want to see them get out of harm's way.

Hardship

Jamal in *Slumdog Millionaire*. Westley in *The Princess Bride*. They were they born into poverty; they never seem to catch a break. We connect with that, we have compassion, and we want to see them succeed in the end.

The Underdog

Harry Potter. Luke Skywalker from *Star Wars*. Forrest Gump. These guys are really inexperienced, fresh-faced and naive. They don't know why but they have a lot of responsibilities. People look up to them, and they have to step up and provide comfort to others. We love them because humans love to see the underdog win.

The Rebel

Jake Sully. John Dunbar in *Dances with Wolves*. Juno. Ferris Bueller. They don't always follow the rules, but through their character arc they come to realize the difference between the choice that is expected and the choice that is right for them. Also, something about their disregard for authority is cool.

Likable Bad Boys

Jack Sparrow in *The Pirates of the Caribbean*. Indiana Jones. Hank Moody in *Californication*. Why do we like the self-absorbed, bad boys and girls? Because they are not like most people we know. They fly by the seat of their pants and do what they please. We might not want to date them in reality, but we love to fawn over them.

Bonding With Your Characters

Pick three of the character bonding tactics listed above and apply them to your characters. How can you use these tactics to improve the reader's relationship with your character?

1. _____

_____

2. _____

_____

3._____

_____

Character Death

We talked about character stakes in the section on middles, but now it's time to figure out what will happen to your character if they are not victorious. If failure doesn't come with a serious threat of death, literal or figurative, the character will not have a reason to succeed. This is where all your practice in making things dire for your character comes to a head. And remember, death can come in many forms—not just the traditional six feet under variety.

Your character may face death in many forms, including:

Professional: Loss of Job, loss of credibility, unemployment, or failure in chosen career

Financial: Loss of wealth, inability to care for self or family

Moral: Unable to stand up for their core values, forced to act against their personal morals.

Obsession: Loss of a place, thing or person with some hold on your character. (The Overlook Hotel in *The Shining* or the Ring in *Lord of the Rings.*)

Actual Death

Relationships: Loss of romance, friendship or parental approval

Psychological: Loss of sanity or control

―――――――――――――――――――――

My character faces Death in the form of: ―――――――――――――――

when she ――――――――――――――――――――――――――

He will overcome these obstacles by: ――――――――――――――――

Character Questionnaire

How well do you know your main character? The better you know your character, the better you can write their story. All of these details don't have to, and probably shouldn't, make it into your story. The questionnaire is meant to help you build your relationship with your characters.

1. What is your character's name? _____

2. Do they have a nickname? _____

3. What is your character's hair color? _____

4. Eye color? _____

5. What are your character's distinguishing physical features? _____

    _____

6. Scars? _____

7. How did they get the scars? _____

    _____

8. Is your character's family present in her life? _____

9. Who is your character closest to? _____

    _____

10. Where was your character born? _____

11. Where is home now? _____

12. What is her biggest fear? _____

13. Does he have a secret? _____

_____

14. What makes your character laugh? _____

_____

15. What are her favorite movies? _____

_____

16. What bands does he listen to? _____

_____

17. What's up next on his MP3 player? _____

18. How much money is in their wallet? _____

19. What are the last five charges to their debit card? _____

_____

_____

20. When is the last time they went to the mall? _____

21. If he had a pet turtle, what would its name be? _____

22. Who was your character's first love? _____

23. Are they still in contact? _____

24. Is your character in love now? _____

25. It's time to clean out the garage, is it easy or hard for him to throw things away?

_____

26. What would your character keep? _____

_____

27. It's Thursday at 3:00pm. Where is your character and what are they doing?

_____

28. What is your character's favorite childhood memory? _____

_____

29. Who was her best friend in high school? _____

30. What does your character do to relax? _____

31. What book is on his night stand? _____

32. What does she consider her greatest achievement? _____

_____

33. What is her current state of mind? _____

_____

34. If he could travel anywhere, where would it be? _____

35. When and where was your character the happiest? _____

_____

36. What does she regret? _____

_____

37. What is the quality they like most in a woman? _____

38. What is the quality they like most in a man? _____

39. Who are their fictional heroes? _____

_____

40. Which living person do they most admire? _____

41. What would cause them to lie? _____

_____

42. Does she have overused phrases and words? _____

_____

Turning Your Ideas into a Novel

Asking Why

If the writer has one duty that is most important when they sit down to write or analyze the world at large, it's to ask "Why?" at every opportunity. Good writing does not come from half-assed interpretation of the world at large, but through careful observation of the world around you and reinterpretation through your words. So keep asking why, all the time, at every turn.

When you're writing, ask yourself, "Why is my character about to open that door? Why is he quitting his job?"

When you're walking to the grocery store and see a vagrant, ask yourself why he's there or what led him to that situation.

When building your scenes, ask why it's raining, why the character is in that place and where they are going from there.

Professional Lying and Stealing

There's no way around it; writing fiction is telling lies. You take a story and mold it, twist it to your concepts and themes. You create a person, place, circumstances, history, plot, all to draw the reader in and lie to them—convince them that what they are reading is real and true. You want them to believe in your characters and care about them as much as you do. One of the best ways to achieve this is by telling the truth.

I promise I'm not talking in circles. Start with something you and your readers both know to be true and stretch it, skew it, or turn it on its head. Take the basics of the human condition and recreate them through your story and characters. Base the attitude, the voice or the hair of your main character on your favorite barista or your first grade teacher or your best friend, but then change these things to fit your character and story.

You can do this with more than just characters. You can use situations and events in the same way. If your acquaintance's friend loses a limb in a freak circus accident, steal the idea and make it your own. Instead of losing a limb, have the character lose a few fingers or even die. Take situations from the news, from your office or your mommy playgroup, and then lie. Change the circumstances and details.

Make a list of some character traits you can steal from at least three interesting people.

1. Person: _____

Trait: _____

2. Person: _____

Trait: _____

3. Person: _____

Trait: _____

Now do the same for situations from your life or the news:

1. Event: _____

_____

2. Event: _____

_____

3. Event: _____

_____

Author Source

Years ago, I was in a writing group with a wide age range. I was in my early twenties, our oldest member was in her forties, and our youngest, Mark, was seventeen. One day Mark vented his frustration to the group about the question we've all had to deal with: "What are you writing?" One of the guys in the group quipped, "Just tell them you're writing about the human condition. That's all they need to know."

We all laughed, because it's true. Fiction, whether movies, novels or television, is about what it means to be human: our experiences, how we interact with them, and how we make sense of it all. I love being human. There's something fascinating about the depths of depression, the throes of passion and even the tedium of going to work. Those moments make great fiction.

By now I'm sure you've heard the phrase "write what you know" a million times. I think "write who you are" is a better guide to compelling and successful writing. Your own personal experiences and emotions are fertile ground to find excellent plots and characters. Unless you have nothing in common with anybody in the world, writing who you are will help your story and your characters become something readers can relate to. When I'm drawn to song lyrics it's usually because I think "I've felt that exact same thing before!" and that's what you want your readers to think too.

"Every author in some way portrays himself in his works, even if it be against his will."
Goethe

Write Who You Are

What is most important to you? _____

How would you want your epitaph to read? _____

What do you like and dislike about your physical appearance? _____

_____

How do your flaws affect you? _____

What are your strengths of character? _____

Who would you most like to be compared to? _____

What do you fear most? _____

What do you wish you were good at? _____

_____

What are some of your more annoying habits? _____

_____

What secret do you hope is never revealed? _____

What is your favorite part of the human condition? _____

_____

Memoir versus Fiction

Writing memoir isn't just for famous people anymore, as demonstrated by recent bestsellers and movies. *Julie & Julia* and *Eat, Pray, Love* are just two of many well-known examples. We're drawn to the human emotion of fiction by the same force that draws us to the reality of other people's lives.

All writers have experiences and your experiences are going to color the stories you write. In fact, I have already told you several times to use your own life as inspiration. That doesn't make it a memoir, though. Memoir is the creative, but factual, telling of your personal and experiences. There are many wonderful books about writing memoir, and this is not one of them. This book is about writing fiction, which is the creative and realistic, but *not* factual, telling of stories.

Where's the line?

Ask James Frey. His book *A Million Little Pieces* is about his own struggle through addiction. After Oprah picked it for her book club, it came out that he had changed several details of his life story to make a more interesting read. Oprah ripped him apart on her show after learning the truth, and his name became synonymous with faking a memoir. Most of what Oprah had loved about the book was true, but she and her viewers felt lied to. The trust between the writer and reader was shattered.

If you're going to present your story as memoir you had better have your facts straight. What are the facts? Facts are the events as they happened, the places and people in the stories. The smoking gun in Frey's case was the amount of time spent in jail. You can't fudge details like that and still call it memoir. If you want to fictionalize your story, go ahead, but call it fiction. Charles Bukowski is a great example of someone who didn't want to deal with facts. He created a character named Hank Chinaski, which allowed him to write whatever he wanted without having to present the facts, even though his stories are widely known to be autobiographical.

What are not facts? Things like the color of the shirt you were wearing, the way your husband smiled when your daughter was born or the way you felt at your mother's death bed. These are details that can be embellished or adjusted to help the readers connect to your story without changing the facts. Creative non-fiction is like a realistic painting; it depicts things as they are, but with an artistic take on the situation. A good memoir should read like a novel, drawing the reader into the character (you) as you tell your story.

Noun Association

Ray Bradbury is known for keeping lists of nouns that popped into his head. I love this concept, because it's something everybody can do. Words get stuck in my head like catchy songs. I often wonder why my brain repeats the same words over and over, but I've taken to writing them down as they come. These words can lead to other words, and before you know it you'll be associating. This exercise can help you find new ideas or drudge up memories you hadn't thought of in years.

Write down a list of nouns and a quick description of a time, event or place that they remind you of.

Examples:

Teacups—Grandma's Kitchen

Rain—Preschool

Coffee—Ben

"*You must stay drunk on writing so reality cannot destroy you.*"
Ray Bradbury

Mindmapping

I'm a very visual person. I can't follow directions without a map. I enjoy both reading and writing because I can see the words and story unfolding on the page. I can't follow a story in audiobook. If you are a visual learner like me, Mindmapping can be a great technique for developing your ideas. Start with a single thought or concept in the center of the page, then branch out from it with related concepts. Try it with any scene or question, cluster certain ideas together and just follow your brain's patterns.

[Scene or Character]

Writing Exercises

Sometimes you need to write to get the ideas flowing. Try a couple of these writing exercises to get to know your characters and story.

Using nothing but dialogue, write a scene between your character and the most important person in their life...

_____

_____

_____

_____

_____

_____

_____

_____

_____

_____

_____

_____

Writing Exercises

Write a scene based on one of the major plot-points in your story from the perspective of someone who is not your main character...

_____

_____

_____

_____

_____

_____

_____

_____

_____

_____

_____

_____

Writing Exercises

    Google the name of the city your character grew up in, and write a short scene based on the first image you see...

_____

_____

_____

_____

_____

_____

_____

_____

_____

_____

_____

Writing Exercises

    Your character has just stepped onto a subway in New York. Write about the experience...

_____

_____

_____

_____

_____

_____

_____

_____

_____

_____

_____

Writing Exercises

Write a scene from the perspective of the main character's pet...

_____

_____

_____

_____

_____

_____

_____

_____

_____

_____

_____

Your character wakes up. Describe the state of their room...

_____

_____

_____

_____

_____

_____

_____

_____

_____

_____

_____

Writing Exercises

Describe, in detail, the setting for the opening scene of your novel...

_____

_____

_____

_____

_____

_____

_____

_____

_____

_____

Ready to Write?

Does Your Idea Measure Up?

We've covered the basics of taking your story from an idea to a first draft, and after you've gone through the process you'll start to realize that not every idea is golden. Even if you choose not to pursue an idea, I don't recommend throwing any of them out, because you never know when they might be useful. Always hold on to your creativity—as long as it's in a healthy, sane way that doesn't land you on the television show *Hoarders*. Keep everything you come up with in a notebook or on your computer. You might be surprised to discover in a year or two (or ten) that you have something in there you really love.

Take your favorite idea, the one you're most excited to write about, and ask the following questions:

- Does my story have fire? YES ____ NO ____

- Can this story sustain itself? YES ____ NO ____

- Do I have the passion to keep it going? YES ____ NO ____

- Will my content keep the reader engaged? YES ____ NO ____

- Should I expand upon my ideas? YES ____ NO ____

- Does my story have hidden potential? YES ____ NO ____

- Does my story stand out? YES ____ NO ____

- Can I create dynamic situations for my characters? YES ____ NO ____

Has this story been done before?

YES _____ NO _____ Of course it has, but not like this! _____

How can you make it different?

_____

_____

Is the setting ordinary?

YES _____ NO _____ Yes, but it's on purpose! _____

How can you make the setting more interesting?

_____

_____

Are my characters boring or stereotypical?

YES _____ NO _____ Yes, but it's on purpose! _____

How can you freshen the characters to make them interesting and easy to relate to?

_____

_____

Is this story "big enough" to interest a substantial number of people?

YES _____ NO _____

How can you widen the story's reach?

_____

_____

Will a large audience understand the story and be engaged?

YES _____ NO _____

Are there any elements that will add to reader fascination and interest?

_____

_____

Choosing Tools and Creating Rituals

The right tools can make the difference between success and frustration. Which you use to write is your own choice. There's no universal tool that will make it easier to write your novel, because each person is different. Some people choose to write on their father's old typewriter, others like to use a basic text program on their computer, some use paper and pen and others use programs like Scrivener . This choice is completely yours.

Writing rituals are important habits that will get you started and keep you motivated to write. Your ritual may include what time of the day you write, where you write, what you wear or what you listen to while you write. When you find something that brings your brain to the place where you're ready to write, make it a part of your ritual. That could be a certain coffee shop, an album you put on repeat or a scarf you wear every time. Habits aren't formed automatically; you have to make them habits.

I plan and plot on paper, but when I'm actually writing I use Microsoft Word on a laptop . I also like raspberry mochas, pugs, Tegan & Sara, Indian food and my blue Kia Sportage. That doesn't mean that you need to like these things.

Knowing what other people do can help you understand your options, but there is no reason to emulate other people if their methods don't work for you—even if it's your favorite writer. Try everything until you find the combination that makes you the most comfortable.

Assessing and Adjusting Your Goals

Once you start writing, you're going to realize you are ahead of your goals on some days and behind on others. Sometimes life is completely unkind and dumps problem after problem in your lap before you can react, let alone write.

So, what do you do once you realize that you're three weeks behind the original goal you set? You reevaluate the time frame and reset your expectations. If you're three weeks behind, change your daily goal to 1500 words instead of 1200 and make up the time. If that's not possible, change your deadline. You made these goals in the first place and the only person you're accountable to is yourself. Finishing this book is something that you *want,* so make time for it—and yourself. On several occasions, I've written 10,000 words a day for three days in a row to make up for lost time. When that happened, I made writing my priority, set aside the time and made sure I had a lot of caffeine on hand. Figure out your limits, overcome your obstacles and reach your goals.

If you find yourself constantly falling behind and changing your goal, find a confidant who will hold you accountable. This person doesn't even have to be a writer—it's often better if they aren't because writers can enable each other to miss goals through commiseration. Your confidant can be your friend, your sibling, your teacher, your barista, your child, your partner, your mail man, your co-worker, your boss, your pet groomer or your babysitter. The point is to find someone you see regularly, so that every time you see them they will ask "How is the writing going? Are you on target?" This small motivation can be enough to keep you going until the day you can say "Absolutely! I've finished my first draft!"

Are You Ready? Checklist

My daily writing goal is: _____

☐ I have a dynamic main character!

☐ I know what my character's goal is!

☐ I know what my character's opposition is!

☐ I know where my story is going to start!

☐ I have a basic plan for the character's journey!

☐ I have a unique setting!

☐ I have set aside time to write!

☐ I have friends and resources for when I get stuck!

☐ I have achievable goals!

While Writing

"She could, she thinks, have entered another world. She could have had a life as potent and dangerous as literature itself."
Michael Cunningham, *The Hours*

I'm Stuck, Now What?

Questions to Ask Yourself

By this point, you're halfway through your manuscript and you've come to read this section because you ran into a brick wall and remembered it was here. However, I know that, like me, most people read through books chronologically and you're probably continuing on from the previous section. But pretend with me that you're stuck and you're 30,000 words into a great novel.

I don't believe in writer's block. I think it's an excuse that people make when they are doubt themselves, tired, lazy or looking for a reason to skip writing and go out to the park. Writing is a matter of physically touching keys on a keyboard or picking up a pen. It can be mentally exhausting, but you can always do it. Like walking—sometimes you're tired and you don't want to walk, but you can. No matter how tired you are, you can always stand up and walk to your bed. You can always write.

To quote Ken Davis, a writer and friend of mine, "People only fail when they quit." This is completely true. If you do not quit, you can't fail. This applies to most things in life, but particularly in writing and publishing. You think you're stuck? You think you have writer's block? Start asking questions. I talked about this before, but now in the thick of writing is when it is most helpful.

Questions to ask if you're facing character & plot frustrations:

Why is your character in this situation? _____

_____

How can they get out? _____

_____

Where are they going from here? _____

_____

Where are the side characters? _____

_____

When is the last time you checked in on your opposition?

_____

_____

And always: How can you make things worse for your character?

_____

_____

Questions to ask if you're facing emotional writer's block:

As generally self-deprecating artists, we all have bad days. Some days it seems like there's no point to finishing the manuscript, article or poem that we're working through. Sometimes it feels like no one else wants us to finish either.

When you face these emotional challenges, ask yourself the following questions:

What is causing me to struggle? _____

_____

Am I facing a particularly daunting section or scene? _____

_____

How can I reward myself for finishing what I set out to do? _____

_____

Why did I want to write this book in the first place? _____

_____

What will I regret if I walk away from this project? _____

_____

How will I feel when I finish? _____

_____

Reaching out to your Community

In today's day and age we're lucky to have the internet readily available, which allows us to connect in ways that we never have before. Sometimes when you're drowning all you need is a friendly voice to pull you out, and that voice is easier to find because we can network with friends and colleagues or join online groups for writers.

Writers are a special kind of human being. Have you ever noticed the deflated feeling that invades your brain when you run up to your non-writer wife, husband or dog and try to explain a scene or the joy of completing a character arc to them? It's not their fault—don't hold it against them. They don't get it because they aren't writers. You love them for many reasons, but you still need that connection to other writers. Go out and find them.

Build relationships; let others know that you're writing and looking for fellowship. Join a local writer's association. Here in Washington State we have the Pacific Northwest Writers Association and it's huge. Search the internet to find similar local or national organizations. You might have to drive a little, but it's worth it for the fellowship. Camaraderie is a basic human need and you should go out of your way to fulfill this need so you can keep writing.

Online Resources

Another benefit of living in this era is the availability of online support systems, prompts and communities. I've listed a few of my favorites below.

Oneword.com

One Word is a quick writing prompt that only allows you 60 seconds to write. They post one word per day, and it can be an excellent jump start.

Typetrigger.com

This is just like One Word, but cooler because it allows more space for writing and has several new prompts per day.

Redbubble.com

Red Bubble is a community art and writing site. They have many different styles of visual art. I often search for a keyword I am writing about and make the picture I find my desktop wallpaper.

NaNoWriMo.org

This is the home of National Novel Writing Month. You can visit the forums for inspiration and local events during November.

#writechat or #amwriting on Twitter

Two excellent communities of writers gather and talk about the craft on Twitter. Search for the hashtags #writechat or #amwriting to read recent conversations or join in!

Dealing with Distractions

My life is full of distractions. My cellphone rings twenty-five times a day, I have emails coming in constantly, my kids need me and my pets occasionally need food. I leave the house when I need to write. As I said earlier, I work well in my office, but I *write* well at a coffee shop.

There are times when you need to leave, or shut the door to your writing space. Or ask your husband to take the dog for a walk. This is your prerogative. Don't let guilt keep you from doing what you must. You are a human being before you're a wife, husband, employee, daughter, son or mother. There are times when you need time for yourself and your writing, and taking this time doesn't make you a bad person.

With that said, we all have responsibilities and distractions. I can't write when there's email in my inbox. I have to respond before I can allow my brain to access the creative. There's no magic solution here. You have to figure out what your priorities are, how to stack them against your creative needs and still feed your fish, take out the garbage and go to work. If something works well, do it again. If writing at a coffee shop is a huge distraction, don't do it. This seems simple, but it's the truth. Every writer is different; you might have to continue to experiment for yourself.

Celebrating Victories

An important part of setting goals is celebrating when you achieve them. Give yourself some credit! If you hit your end goal, or even your halfway mark, allow yourself the victory. Post about it online, go to dinner or just bask in the sense of accomplishment. Goals are guideposts for your journey, so take time to enjoy the rest stops and mile markers.

Getting Over a Bad Days

Along with responsibilities, we all have bad days (and weeks and months). Some days you just can't write. There have been times when I've set aside specific days or times to write, but when I sit at the keyboard I find myself pulling out my hair in fits of frustration. There's a part of me that wants to run when this happens. I dream of a "normal" life. A life in which I wake up, watch the *Today* show, spend time with my family and end the day with some more mindless television. I have other secret dreams about running off, working at Starbucks and attending art school. As much as I'd like to fantasize about it, though, I can't give up writing. When I shower, drive, walk the dog or pick the kids up from school, I'm writing in my head. I'm creating stories, settings and characters. Even if I finally gave up writing professionally, I don't think I'd ever stop. This seems to be a trait common to all writers.

So what do you do when you want to give up?

Take a break. Allow yourself a night to play board games, go out with your friends or watch *American Idol*. Just like any job, you are entitled to take a day off now and then. Your manuscript will still be waiting for you tomorrow.

If you're on a deadline, or behind on personal goals, break your current task into several smaller pieces. Need to make 2,500 words before bed? Challenge yourself to 500 words at a time. Once you meet a goal, reward yourself. Out at your favorite coffee shop? Treat yourself to an extra whipped-mocha-chocolate something or other. At home? Indulge in extra time with your cat or dinner at the table with your spouse (a rather novel idea for the frazzled writer, I know).

Talk to someone. This could be a friend, girlfriend or writing partner. Let them know you're struggling. Venting your frustration is a great way to get over a problem; it works wonders for me. You will feel less alone when you have someone on your side as encouragement.

Do not give up. You started writing for a reason. If you're facing the dark depths of despair, write down the reason you started writing your novel. Stick that reminder on your monitor, above your desk, on your fridge, on your friend, on your desk at work (be cryptic if your reason includes "quit this stupid job") or anywhere you might look when you need encouragement.

Am I Actually Done?

When I wrote my first novel, I think I announced that I was "done" seven or eight times. It's still not done, and the truth is it will never be done, but it was a great learning experience for me as a writer. If we allowed ourselves, we'd futz with our novels forever. Hand-in-hand with celebrating victories, you should understand the process. Once you reach the end of your first draft, you've met the first major goal, but now the hard work starts.

Just like your muscles strengthen with exercise, your writing will get stronger as you move through your novel, so I suggest that you do one-and-a-half first drafts. This may sound silly, but as you reach the end of your first draft, go right back to the beginning of the story. This will help you start to write a vivid, well-crafted beginning, because your character's voice and writing style will still be strong from writing the end of the story.

After Writing

"Let me live, love and say it well in good sentences."
Sylvia Plath

Revision & Editing

The Difference between Revision and Editing

Congratulations! You're done! You've completed your first draft (or, if you took my advice, your first-draft-and-a-half).Now it's time to take a second look at what you've written and enter the revision phase. It might feel nice to take off your writing hat for a while, but do not be fooled—there's still a lot of writing in your future.

What is the difference between revising and editing your manuscript?

Both are important parts of the post-first draft process, but are very different from one another. Revision literally means re-envisioning your draft. It is your chance to fill in gaps and check your pacing, tone and continuity. Editing, on the other hand, is the process of searching for and correcting sentence structure, grammar and language mistakes.

If you try to grammar-edit your piece without revising first, you're liable to miss major parts of the manuscript or have to repeat your work. Grammar editing is not fun for most people (and if you enjoy grammar editing your own manuscript, you might be a masochist). Save yourself some headaches and work on your structure, dialogue and character development first.

Anton Chekhov advised setting aside your manuscript for a year. A full year! Can you imagine spending all that time writing your first draft only to ostracize your lovingly crafted characters into a drawer for a year? Yeah, I can't either.

However, I do understand the sentiment, and I do believe you need breaks between revisions/drafts. A month or two works perfectly for me; I come back with fresh eyes on everything I've written. This is another situation where you have to learn what works best for you. If you're itching to start revision and might explode if you don't get going, then do it. You're the artist. Don't risk losing your drive over an arbitrary number, but if you can handle the separation anxiety, try to set your manuscript aside for a month or so before starting the process.

The Revision Process

There's a strategy to revision. My first step is to read the entire manuscript without making any changes. The best way to do this is on an e-reader if you have one, because you don't have the option to edit as you go. Put the entire document on a Nook or Kindle and read without stopping to edit. Who cares if that comma is in the wrong place? You'll catch it later when you're editing. You have one job on the first read-through: you're looking for structure, character development and plot progression.

After you've read the whole draft once, start again from the beginning and this time arm yourself with a pen. I prefer purple; it feels less like I'm being graded. Embrace marginalia, write questions to yourself in the margins. Read like a reader, not like the author. Ask all the same questions I mentioned in the first part of this book.

After you've completed this for all of your chapters (or scenes, or sections), go back to the beginning and read it again without revising. Read, re-envision, change. When you feel your story is as strong as it's going to be, it's time to check it once more.

The Ten Steps Revisited

Now is a great time to revisit the Ten Steps from page thirty.

1. Plot—The Plan
2. Story Pacing
3. Themes and Ideas
4. Realistic and Believable Dialogue
5. Excellent Writing Mechanics
6. Intriguing Setting/Mood/Tone
7. Haunting and Precise Description
8. Compelling and Human Characters
9. Creativity
10. Read, Read, Read

Each one of the steps is even more important and relevant now. Read your story and search for ways to improve your writing with each of these fundamentals. Incorporating these elements will help create a stronger backbone for your book.

10 Steps Checklist Revisited

My plot is: _____

_____

My themes and ideas are: _____

My unique setting and tone are: _____

The most creative thing about my idea is: _____

_____

I am currently reading: _____

My story follows logical pacing: YES ____ NO ____

My story has realistic and believable dialogue: YES ____ NO ____

My writing has excellent grammar and mechanics: YES ____ NO ____

I have haunting and well-written descriptions: YES ____ NO ____

I have compelling characters: YES ____ NO ____

Grammar Editing

By this time you've probably read your piece so many times that you're ready to follow Chekhov's advice and put it away in a drawer for year—or maybe you already have. Once you've stopped hating your novel, it's time to start editing. This is a tricky step for most writers. You've spent so much time in your manuscript, reading, writing, revising and re-writing so many times that you have probably found yourself changing something and then changing it back again on the next pass. Yes, we all do it. But through this process you've developed your plot and refined your character arcs, and now it's time to focus on the mechanics of grammar.

We all wish that we were born with the ability to produce the perfect sentence on the first try, but to be honest, grammar isn't all there is to writing. Who cares if you can write a perfect, grammatically-correct sentence if you can't tell a good story? Do you think that Scheherazade focused on the grammar of her sentences when she told 1001 stories to keep herself alive? No, because the foundation of good writing is a good story.

So then, why is grammar important?

Grammar is important because it shows your grasp of and respect for language. It makes your meaning perfectly clear, allowing your reader to seamlessly integrate into your story. You never walk away from a well-edited book and tell all your friends about the proper use of commas, but if you read something with many grammar mistakes it draws your focus away from the story and sticks with you . You want to hook your reader, not drive them away.

Common Grammar Mistakes

I've included a list and explanations of common grammar mistakes below. It is by no means a definitive list, but these are the basic mistakes that can shatter the credibility of a manuscript. I have tried to boil the list down to simple, easy to understand terms. I've heard many, many times how difficult some grammar rules can be to follow. If you want to learn more, there are plenty of really good grammar books, including *Self Editing for Fiction Writers* which I read many years ago and enjoyed—as much as one can enjoy a grammar book.

Run-on Sentences

Run-on sentences are created when you have two separate subject/verb combinations in one sentence. These are easy to spot. Read the portion before the "and" and again after it. If each of these statements could stand alone as a sentence, it's a run-on.

Example: Sally went to the store and she purchased some dried apples.

Fix: Sally went to the store. She purchased some dried apples. *OR* Sally went to the store, and she purchased some dried apples. *OR* Sally went to the store and purchased some apples.

Comma Splices

A comma splice occurs when a comma splits a sentence in half. This can be caused by a missing conjunction (as in the example) or just a gross misuse of commas.

Example: Sally loved dried apples, she ate them every day for breakfast.

Fix: Sally loved dried apples. She ate them every day for breakfast. *OR* Sally loved dried apples and ate them every day for breakfast. *OR* Sally loved dried apples, and she ate them every day for breakfast.

Sentence Fragments

A basic sentence forms when you have a subject and a verb: *Sally* (noun/subject) *eats* (verb) *dried apples.* If you do not have both primary elements of a sentence, you end up with a fragment. In creative writing, fragments *can* be used sparingly for emphasis, but you should be careful about littering your manuscript with them.

Example: John stepped out of the car. Walked forward.

Fix: John stepped out of the car and walked forward.

Introductory Clauses

Often sentences begin with an introductory clause, and these clauses should be followed by a comma. The clause includes information relevant to the sentence; however the sentence could stand alone without it.

Examples: As I was reading your piece, I thought about my mother.

Looking up, Sarah saw a cat on the windowsill.

Dangling Participle

A participle is a verb in present (–ing) or past (usually –ed) tense, used to describe a noun. "Looking up" is a participle in the sentence above. A participle is dangling when it is not connected to the noun doing the action it describes.

Example: Running to catch a bus, her apple got lost.

Fix: She lost her apple while running to catch a bus. *OR* Running to catch a bus, she lost her apple.

Pronoun/Antecedent Agreement

A pronoun is used to substitute for a noun, and an antecedent is the noun it refers to. In the sentence "Sally went to the store, and she purchased some dried apples," the pronoun is "she" and Sally is the antecedent. If you use the wrong pronoun or your pronoun doesn't have a clear antecedent, you will confuse your readers.

Example: Sally ate the apples and it was delicious.

Fix: Sally ate the apples and they were delicious. *OR* Sally ate the apple and it was delicious

Example: Sally and Jessica love to pick apples from her apple tree.

Fix: Sally and Jessica are friends. They love to pick apples from Jessica's apple tree.

Passive Voice

You're using active voice when the subject of your sentence acts, and passive voice when the subject is acted on. It's easy to slip into writing in passive voice; it's how we talk to each other. This is appropriate sometimes, but in most cases it's best to use active language. Creative writing should engage the reader, and passive voice puts distance between the reader and the page. Using passive voice can also add bulk to your sentences.

This was a problem of mine for years, and I think passive voice might be the biggest issue for most writers I know. They hear about it all the time, but do not know how to fix it. I'm going to try my hardest to explain passive voice in the easiest to understand way. I finally mastered it, and you can too.

Example: Shane **had been exhausted** by working in the garage for hours.
Fix: Shane exhausted himself working in the garage.
Example: Over the din I **was not forced** to fake a conversation.
Fix: Over the din, I did not have to fake conversation.

Semicolons

One of my pet peeves is the overuse or misuse of semicolons. Very few people actually know how to use them; I'm not one of those people. The Oatmeal (an entertainment website based in Seattle) has a great comic on semicolons and you should look it up, right now. If, like me, you aren't sure how to use semicolons correctly, read his comic until you have it memorized.

Some correct uses for the semicolon:

Connecting two independent clauses with similar themes (a semicolon should never be used to connect clauses that cannot stand as individual sentences and should never be used with a conjunction like, and, or, but), or to break up a list with extraneous punctuation.

Example: Sarah stopped skipping breakfast; she eats an apple every morning.
Example: I love Sylvia Plath, a poet; *The Virgin Suicides*, a literary fiction novel; and Indian food.

One Space after a Period

Double-spacing was necessary in the past to make new sentences stand out in typewritten text. It's not 1964 and most of us are not typing on manual typewriters. It's time to give up the habit of double spacing after a period. With the evolution of the computer we don't have to create that extra space between sentences any more, and it drives typographers crazy. I know this may come as a shock, and no, I don't care if Mrs. Looney taught you the other way around. If you absolutely cannot give up this habit, do a "Find and Replace" in your word processing program. Type a double-space in the Find box and replace it with a single space.

Unintentional Repetition of Certain Words and Phrases

I do this all the time in first drafts. It's easy to do, especially if you are distracted in the middle of the sentence.

Example: Tori walked to the counter and set her purse on the counter.

Yes, we get it, there's a counter there (this is an actual example from the first draft of *Inked*). Watch for this type of repetition when you revise.

Another thing writers accidentally do in drafts is repeat certain words. Sometimes it can be used deliberately for effect, but most often it's a lack of imagination or focus. I once had someone proofread a first draft, and I used the word "dark" (or a synonym) thirty-seven times in one chapter. I used the word so many times that he counted, just to make a point, and if he was counting the number of "darks," how was he paying attention to the story?

Missing/Extra Words

As you start to edit and revise, you'll change sentence structure and move words around. This can potentially lead to missing words or repeated words. These are usually short words that we don't pay attention to, but readers tend to notice when they're missing. This is why a second pair of eyes (or ten) on your draft is so important. If you've read a sentence forty-two times and didn't see the missing "at" or the double "the" you're probably not going to see it on read forty-three.

Colloquialisms

We have all grown up saying things in certain ways. I lived in Georgia for a year, and I laughed every time I heard someone refer to a shopping cart as a buggy. It's important to know if your language choices are regional. If you live in Georgia and your story is set in New York, you should check your wording with someone from that area.

Even if your phrases are right for the setting, be careful about mangling figures of speech. Most people say "I could care less" to show how little something matters to them. The correct saying is "I could not care less." Another of my favorite misused sayings is "Once and awhile." The correct use saying is "Once in a while". There's a certain amount of time (a while) and something happens once in that period. As a writer, you may decide that a mangled phrase like "I could care less" represents your character's personality. This can be an effective way to develop your character, as long as it's done intentionally. You don't want your readers second-guessing your credibility.

Commonly Misspelled/Misused Words

Your/You're—Your is a possessive pronoun. If you say "your face," referring to that person's face. If it belongs to you, it is your dog, your car, your purse. "You're" is a contraction of "you are." The easiest way to avoid misusing contracted forms of words is to try it without the apostrophe. If you're typing "You're a dork," say it aloud: "You are a dork." You'll be able to recognize that "You're face is red" is wrong because "You are face is red" doesn't work.

There/Their/They're—"There" is a place, as in "I heard about a sale at the mall. Let's go there." However, "their" is possessive: their house, their coffee, their job. "They're" is a contracted form of "they are." Just like the previous contraction, say the full words if you struggle with the difference. "They're going to the store" is correct. "They're car is red" is not.

Who's/Whose—"Who's" is the contracted form of "who is" or "who has." "Who's at the concert tonight?"—"Who is at the concert tonight?" or "Who's been to the theater before?"—"Who has been to the theater before?"

"Whose" is another possessive pronoun. "Whose car is that?" is correct. "Who is car is that?" wouldn't work in the sentence.

Its/It's—"It's" is a contracted form of "it is" or "it has." "It's dark out there."—"It is dark out there." Or "It's been a dark night."—"It has been a dark night."

Use "its" to show possession: "The chameleon changed its color to match the leaves" is correct because the color belongs to the chameleon. "The chameleon changed it is color" doesn't work.

Then/Than—"Then" shows the order of events: "Put on your socks, then your shoes." "Than" compares one thing to another: "A whale is larger than a seahorse" or "I have less money than Bill Gates."

Every Writer Needs an Editor

It's absolutely true, every writer in the world needs an editor. I don't care if you're Stephen King or Toni Morrison—you need an editor. You need as many eyes as you can get on your book.

I put out the first edition of *Inked* in a hurry. Looking back, I realize I didn't need to publish it so quickly. I made many mistakes in the first stages of indie authorship, but my biggest mistake was not hiring an external editor. Thank goodness, there are only about fifty copies of the first edition running around out there in the world.

After four or five months, I realized that I wasn't happy with the writing. I had grown as a writer while working on other projects, and I had never set the manuscript aside during revision. When I picked *Inked* up again and read it, I started to feel that it was a poor reflection of my writing skills. I quickly pulled sales of the book and hired an editor, but I wasn't fast enough.

Someone on goodreads.com got a copy of the first edition and left scathing comments about the book because of the grammar mistakes. She did not care that I was fixing it. She went to Amazon.com and gave my book a one-star review, the only one-star review my book has ever received. You don't know creative pain until someone, with all their internet anonymity, rips apart your book. I cried for days. Since I had already pulled the book from production while the editor had it, I was tempted to just cancel sales all together. I faced some of my darkest days as a writer during that time.

When it comes down to it, who can I blame but myself? I put out a book that wasn't completely done or ready for readers. You can still go to Amazon.com and read that one-star review right now. I'm sharing because it's a testament to the mistakes I made, mistakes I will never make again. You should learn from my mistakes.

In the end, the manuscript came back from the editor, polished and beautiful, and I knew I was ready to put it back out there.

Time for a Professional

When is it time to pull in a professional editor? After you've done everything you can to improve your draft, which, by the way, has now graduated to a full-fledged manuscript. First, you have to decide what type of editor you want to employ. There are several options, from "I know a guy with an English degree who is looking to pick up freelance work" to professional book doctors and editors.

Your editing choices will probably be determined by your pocket book. Having your friend's brother-in-law who is an English major will result in the lowest bottom line. You're going to have to take his potentially flawed opinions and advice, but it's better than no editor at all. You can also check classified ads online, ask around in your writers group, look up book doctors or contact your local writing and editing guilds.

Before you part with your hard-earned money, ask the editor to look over several pages and give an example of the feedback they will give. Some other details you should hammer out before money is exchanged are turnaround time, total price, what kind of feedback you're looking for and whether the editor is willing to go over the changes with you after all is said and done.

How to Give and Get Critical Feedback

In today's day and age, you're not going to get anything if you're not offering something in return. If you have people willing to read for you, you should be prepared to read their short stories and manuscripts, and in turn give feedback on what you've read.

Remember when your mother told you "If you can't say something nice, don't say anything at all?" This is not true for writing feedback. The worst piece of feedback to get is "I liked it." When I hear this I cringe because I know I'll be struggling to extract information with questions like "Why? What did you like? What did you think of the characters?"

Do not become that kind of critique partner. If your partner, buddy, co-worker asked you to review their manuscript, do them the kindness of giving actual feedback.

How? Ask questions. Remember all the questions at the beginning of this book? Ask them about the manuscript as you're reading. A few examples would be: *What is happening? What is the Character, Goal, Conflict, Resolution in this chapter/scene/arc?*

When reading someone else's piece for review, keep a log of questions. But, under no circumstances should you show your notes to your partner. They aren't always going to be nice. If the author really wants them, type your notes out and re-word them in a more constructive way when necessary.

Always sandwich your feedback. Start with something positive—yes, there's always something positive to say. After something you liked about the piece, move into what confused you or caused conflict when you were reading. Be specific; instead of saying "I hated this" or "That was a terrible way to portray this event," identify the part you had trouble with, and give suggestions to improve it. Think of it like critique-karma (this concept will come up again when I talk about review-karma, publishing-karma and platform-karma) and give the feedback in a way you'd want to hear it. This is their art, so be careful about the way you criticize.

When receiving feedback it's important to keep an open mind. The most frustrating person on the other end of a critique is the defensive "but it has to be this way because" person. If someone gives you advice, listen to it. It doesn't mean that you have to implement their advice, but listen with an open heart and mind—not a defensive one.

Beta Readers

At this stage of the game, you're ready to reach out and find "Beta Readers." This term comes from software testing, and it means the last line of people to try something out before it is released to the general public. You're going to take your finished, revised and edited manuscript and ask a few select readers to give you feedback on your final piece.

I suggest ten—yes ten—fresh readers, people who have never read your manuscript.

These people can be coworkers, friends, relatives or people in your critique group. When you reach out to them, let them know that you're in the final stages. Prepare a list of questions you can send to them after they read your piece. These questions should be specific to your novel, about your characters and plot points. Don't be scared to ask away!

Revision Checklist

☐ I've read and re-read my manuscript.

☐ I've checked for common grammar mistakes.

☐ I've had at least one editor read over and revise my manuscript.

☐ I've put the manuscript away for at least a month, and then I read it again.

☐ I checked *again* for common grammar mistakes.

☐ I've had at least ten beta readers, and I listened to their feedback and implemented any changes into my manuscript.

☐ I read the manuscript once more.

Publication

"We have to continually be jumping off cliffs and developing our wings on the way down."
Kurt Vonnegut, Jr.

Publishing Options

What do you want to do with your book?

There comes a point in every author's journey where they have to decide which path they will take. Everyone wants The Big Publishing Deal; that's no secret. If the president of Random House knocked on your door and asked for your manuscript, you'd hand it over and take the check.

Unfortunately this dream isn't going to come true for everyone. It's a lot like playing the lottery. I think many writers assume that someone will read their manuscript, love it and publish the book for them. It just doesn't work like that.

Traditional publishing has been the primary route to seeing your book in print for decades. You write a manuscript, query agents until you sign with one, and then they sell your book to someone in New York. If you were unable to get an agent, you were unable to be published. This methodology led to the big-box bookstores and big-name authors we've all heard of. This process worked great for large publishing houses because it meant that agents acted as the gatekeepers. They only brought the best of the best to publishers. The problem with this system is that there are a lot of writers, and as the industry grew agents were hard-pressed to find big publishing houses willing to take risks on something new. They want the same thing that sold last year, another James Patterson thriller or the next *Twilight*.

With the internet and the growth of technology, options for authors unable to find representation—in the traditional sense—have changed.

Small indie presses have been around forever, but Indie presses and the way they operate have changed in the past ten years. With easy access to the internet, apps, and online communities, marketing and distribution options are boundless. Even large retailers like Borders or Barnes & Noble are more accessible, but no longer needed to bring attention to their titles. This means that you, the author, have options. You can go the traditional route, the small press route or you can publish your own book as an independent author.

You have to decide what you want out of publication. Will you only be satisfied by mass-distribution and commercial success? If your answer is yes, then you need to choose the traditional route and ask yourself "Does my book have mass-appeal?" Some books are meant to be indie. The author understands that their storylines and writing style fall outside the realm of Danielle Steel and John Grisham. There's a fine line in commercial success, because you then have to find your own niche without being "tired." No one wants to read a poor rehash of *Animal Farm*, but we do want to read a new take on the theme.

When I stood at the crossroads of publishing options, I thought long and hard about what I wanted from the publication of my book. At first, like most writers, I thought publication would come easy. When the reality of the situation dawned on me, I had to decide what to do about it. Through research, conversations and the reading of many books on publishing, I knew that I could be on the traditional path for a very long time. I imagined myself tromping through a metaphorical jungle with a machete and no end in sight. I started to question my motives for writing in the first place. Was I only in it for the money? How important was the validation of an agent and publisher?

I came to a few very firm conclusions. I wanted my book in print. I wanted people to read it. And if *one* person I'd never met read it and it had an impact, I'd done my job. I realized these were goals I could easily achieve with indie publishing. By the time I had my third review from a complete stranger, I'd met my goal. Brian was my very first fan, and I'll never forget him.

Now, you have to make that choice for yourself.

———————————————————————

What is your book's purpose? ———————————————————————

———————————————————————

What do you want out of publication?———————————————————————

———————————————————————

Traditional Publishing

This is going to be a very quick overview of traditional publishing. There are many books out there on finding agents, writing query letters and how the publishing industry works. I'm covering the basics because I want to clarify the difference between traditional and indie publishing.

What is an Agent?

An agent is your representative, your partner in traditional publishing. They work directly with you and pitch your novel to publishing houses.

Here are a few little-known facts about agents:

1. They are only people. I think it's very important to understand that agents are people too. They like certain manuscripts because they just *do.* An agent at a writer's conference once said that she would have passed on *The Bridges of Madison County,* simply because she didn't like it. So, if one agent rejects your manuscript, move on to the next one. Research the agents you query, make sure that you understand what they represent. They see a lot of queries; don't waste your time or theirs.

2. They only get paid if they can sell your manuscript. An agent will only sign you if they believe they can sell your book. They have to go by the current best-sellers and demand in the market. You might have the best book ever written on father-daughter relationships, but your chances may be ruined if Harper-Collins just launched a very similar book that flopped.

3. They aren't the problem. I know several agents that would love to take on and represent quirky, indie fiction, but if it won't sell they will end up sitting on it. This doesn't do anything for the agent or author. If the big New York Six aren't interested, it's not going anywhere. Obviously there's going to be the occasional one-off situation but it's a risk for them.

4. Finding an agent is not the same as selling your book, especially in the current climate. Most people assume that as soon as they get an agent, that's it—they've hit the big time. Unfortunately, I've heard too many stories of agents unable to sell manuscripts and eventually letting the client out of contract. You're going to have to keep working once you sign on the dotted line. If you choose the traditional method, you should be prepared to listen to your agent because they know what will sell. If you're married to certain unusual aspects of your writing and characters, the traditional method may not be for you.

Pitching Your Novel

To get an agent's attention, you have to pitch your novel. There are different kinds of pitches, but they all basically do the same thing.

There are a few ways to find an agent you can pitch to: query letters, writer's conferences or networking. Query letters are the most common, because you can reach out to someone you've never met before. Writer's conferences are another well-known option, as agents attend for the specific purpose of taking pitches. If you're lucky enough to know "someone who knows someone," don't press your advantage, but do pitch to them if they are asking.

You should be prepared to talk about your book. This isn't as easy as it might seem. You should be able to sum up your book in three sentences—yes that's right, three. But wait, it gets harder. There's also the one sentence pitch. Agents look for this because it shows that you understand your own piece. They will also expect you to understand your genre and your target audience. You should absolutely know these things before you approach any agent.

My friend, who has worked for agents, says that agents have ADD. They are pitched novels and memoirs constantly and you have to grab them in the first few sentences. For this reason it's also important to know what published books are similar to yours.

One Sentence Pitch: _____

_____

Three Sentence Pitch: _____

_____

_____

My Genre: _____

My Comparable Books: _____

_____

My Target Audience: _____

Dealing with Rejection

It's going to come, and you're going to have to learn to deal with it. It sounds harsh, but I'm actually trying to help soften the blow. Do not assume you're going to be any different than everyone else, and everyone in the writing industry deals with it.

So, what do you do when the rejection letters start to come in?

Keep an open mind. Keep sending out queries. Try other types of agents or approaches. Rework your query letter. Most of all, keep writing. You've finished one book, and each book you write is a learning experience. Do not sit on the one project while you wait for fame and fortune. Keep writing and keep perfecting your craft.

There may come a time in your traditional publishing journey when you decide to reevaluate your chosen path. That's your prerogative—no one will judge you, I promise.

Indie Publishing

Don't Give into the Easy Way Out.

The biggest pitfall of indie publishing is the desire to give into the path of least resistance. You can't do this or you will not be successful. It's going to be a lot of work, but it will be worth it.

I mentioned the first cover of *Inked* earlier. I put out red and white vector-art cover that was pretty but completely wrong for my genre. When I saw my book next to other comparable books, mine looked self-published and it was disheartening. I went to the bookstore once a week, pulled every book off the shelf and analyzed the covers. I looked for what I liked, what I didn't like, what worked and what was awful. I took pictures of the covers with my cellphone camera. I realized that all the covers I liked and that made sense with my book were photographic. I was able to take the concepts I loved and execute them myself.

Even if you're going to have a professional design your cover, you have to know what you want. This will take some work and research. If you're working with a small press, you often have the option to be involved with the cover process.

The cover is just the beginning. You should know what you want in every part of the publishing process, because most of it is in your hands. Through my experience I know there will be times you want to take the easy way out. Don't do it. This is your art, your baby, and you want the best for it.

The Pros and Cons of Indie Publishing

From here on, I'll use "indie publishing" in reference to both small press and self-publishing. Most of what I have to say applies to both, and when there's a difference I'll point it out.

Pros:
- Complete artistic control over your piece.

- The ability to market your book the way you want.

- Freedom in layout, design and cover art. If you do choose to seek out small presses, this will be negotiated with your publisher.

- Higher commissions per sale, especially with direct sales.

- The ability to set your own price.

Cons:
- Fewer distribution channels than traditional publishing. (However, the offset is often made up in higher royalties)

- You have to find people to edit, layout and design your book.

- You have to invest your own money up front to hire professionals to do these things for you.

- A lot of hard work and elbow grease.

Working with Small Presses

As the owner of a small press, I can say that I'm in it for the art. Pink Fish Press is a passion project. I realized that there were so many other people in the world with amazing books that would not fit the traditional publishing mold. I wanted to find the best and publish them. Most small presses exist for this same reason.

Like all small press owners, I'm incredibly busy, and it's something to keep in mind when you start to reach out to editors. We might love your piece, but we might also be up to our eyeballs in editing, cover design or marketing other projects. Years ago, a published friend of mine was told by her editor, "Everyone is late in this business." While I don't believe this should always be true, it is an industry built around the hurry-up-and-wait philosophy. So, take a deep breath and recognize that they are only human too. Feel free to reach out to the editors and owners of small presses and ask for a time frame. There's no reason they should not be able to provide an estimated date in which they will read your manuscript, and if they can't–it might be a sign that they are too busy and will not have time to devote to your project. Just like agents, don't put all your eggs in one basket, query several small presses at once until you find the one that works for you.

Finding small presses can also be a challenge. There are directories online, but each one has its own rules and fees and not every small press can be listed. The best way to locate a small press is through word of mouth, local author events and writing associations. When you find a press that you're interested in submitting to, purchase a copy of one of their publications. You need to make sure that you understand what they are publishing, in both content and style, and if they would be a good fit for you.

Understanding what makes a small press different is also important. You're not signing with Random House, and therefore a lot of the responsibility for marketing and publicity is going to fall on you, the author. Your press will want to see you succeed, but they only have so much time and budget to offer. This is true for most new authors, though, at any level of publishing. Large or small, your publisher is going to expect you to blog, market and attend local events to build your platform.

For more information on small presses, read Terry Persun's *Guidebook for Working with Small Independent Publishers*. It's a quick and concise look into working with indie presses based on Terry's personal experiences.

The Financial Stuff

Most people don't have a lot of extra money to invest into publishing their own book. If you choose the indie route, you will need to start thinking about where the money is going to come from.

I do as much as I can with as little money up front as possible, and this requires creative problem solving. This is where networking and finding people whose strengths compliment your weaknesses can be very helpful.

The biggest money-saver these days is Print-on-Demand (POD) technology. This is a service that will print one book at a time as they are ordered. Gone are the days of 2,000-minimum offset print runs. There are a lot of POD services available: two of the biggest are Createspace and Lightning Source. Research various companies and figure out what works for you. POD also allows you more money to spend on graphic designers or layout artists.

Online micro-investment services (such as kickstarter.com) have recently emerged as a way to raise money, however when it comes to writing and publishing fiction it's hard to get other people on board. There's no harm in trying though! Just make sure people can see the potential to get something out of it for themselves.

Another way to get people involved is to offer a percentage of potential profit, or barter your own services for theirs. You may be able to convince someone like an editor, to work on your book for a 10% cut of the sales (or something along those lines).

The dirty truth is that there isn't a lot of money in writing. There are a lot of writers with a lot to say and people seem to be less interested in reading and literary arts. If your expectations are realistic, this shouldn't be a problem. Invest small bits into your art where you can, and remember that your own hard work is always "free." The internet is a great resource; use it and learn to do some things for yourself that you might otherwise have to pay for.

Accepting all your new Roles

Every step in the publishing process has a learning curve, some steeper than others. I often found myself saying "I wish I'd known that!" in my first few months. The great thing about POD is that you can fix things easily (like I did with my cover). Don't let the process frustrate you. Learn what works for you and continue to do those things, and stop doing the things that aren't working. It's not a failure if you try something and find out it doesn't work.

When I first decided to publish my own book I had a hard time coming to terms with my new role. I was a writer, not an editor, graphic designer or marketer. It took me awhile to fully accept these tasks, but if I didn't do them who would? It may be hard at first to reach out and talk about your writing, your body of work and yourself, but it's how you'll sell your book. Prepare yourself now and learn to roll with the punches.

Cover and Interior Design

I already mentioned the importance of your cover, because it's a fact of life that people *do* judge books by their covers. If you feel you can design a cover on your own, you could save a lot of money, but you don't want to have a book that looks "self-published" either.

The same goes for layout, but this one is a lot easier to do on your own. I'm going to frustrate a lot of typographers and book designers with this statement, but it's true: You can design your interior in a word processing program (like Word) to save money. It may not be as professional as a typographer would want, but it's less of a distraction than a crappy cover. If you work hard, study your favorite book's interior, and mess around with settings enough, you can do it without spending several hundred dollars for desktop publishing software like Adobe InDesign.

If you are a student, you probably have access to these programs on-campus, or you can look into other open-source options such as Scribus. There is a pretty steep learning curve with programs like these, and if you can't invest the time into learning how to use them it might be best to pay someone. I think an amazing cover is worth investing money in. It's the first impression people will get of your book, so you absolutely need the layout and design to represent the hard work you've put into it.

Publishing Karma

When you step into the world of publishing, you're going to want people on your side. You'll need people to read and share their opinion of your book, local authors for kudos on the cover and your website, and friends who want to help you succeed (by suggesting your book to their friends, writing reviews and offering moral support). You can get these things by building up your publishing karma.

The internet can be a really harsh place, and you need to be a beneficial part of it. Promote other authors on your Twitter account, celebrate the success of people in your writing group and volunteer at local literacy events. When the time comes to release your book, the people you have helped will want to help you.

As indie authors and publishers we are all working toward the same goals, and there's no reason not to help each other out. Even if it doesn't seem like there's anything in it for you, you have no idea what will happen down the road. Build relationships for the benefit of art and literature as a whole, not just because you want to further yourself.

One of the ways that I do this is through book reviews. I read indie as much as I can, and I give positive reviews when I can. If I can't give a positive review of a book because I just didn't like it, I don't give a bad review—I give no review. Public reviews are not the same as being a beta-reader or reading somebody's draft. To me, no review is just as bad as a negative review, but I'm not running around the internet racking up bad-review-karma that can come back to bite me next time I release a book. Just because I didn't like an indie book doesn't mean that someone else won't, so there's no reason to trash all the work that someone put into their piece.

"Any reviewer who expresses rage and loathing for a novel is preposterous. He or she is like a person who has put on full armor and attacked a hot fudge sundae."
Kurt Vonnegut, Jr.

Platform

Building platform is a necessary task in all types of publishing, but it is especially important for indie authors. You have to find ways to let people know about your book. You do this through networking, online presence, charity functions, volunteer gigs and anything else you can think of.

Many years ago, I volunteered to work with National Novel Writing Month as a Municipal Liaison for the Seattle area. Platform was the farthest thing from my mind when I offered to take on this role, but it's been a great way to integrate myself with the local writing community. Since I started, the size of the group has grown from 2000 to 5,500 at last count. These are all people that I interact with because of the role I took on and invested my time into. When you encounter opportunities like this in your life, take them.

Another way to build platform is through publication in literary journals. It's one of the primary reasons I created *Line Zero*, it's a place where writers of all skill levels can submit and possibly be published. We have a literary contest and publish editorial essays on writing and art. Find magazines and journals that publish in your genre, polish up some of your short pieces and submit. I wouldn't start with *The Paris Review*—start indie while you build your base. Don't limit yourself to just short fiction either, email the editors and as to write a piece on the process, your writing as art or anything else you feel strongly about. Publication is publication, and having any writing in print helps bring credibility to your novel.

Like all aspects of your art, you have to be in it for the right reasons. Don't think that just because you spend one day helping a local youth writing program you'll be rich and sell a million copies of your book. Platform is an ongoing process. Your book will only sell when you work at it, and the moment you stop, so will your sales. Your book might be an amazing piece of fiction, but if no one knows about it, no one will buy it.

So work, blog, volunteer and be an active, positive presence online. If you're writing about a certain topic, find a related community and get involved with them. Teaching is another great way to build your presence and publishing karma; you're sharing what you've learned and helping other writers in the process.

This goes for sales too. If you're talking to an indie author, buy their book. If you want to succeed as an indie writer, why wouldn't you support other artists too?

Social Media

If you had released an independent book twenty years ago, how would you have sold it to people across the country, or even the world? Now, we have the internet and it's pretty awesome. There are many ways to bring your platform and book to readers all over the globe.

Twitter, Facebook, MySpace, GoodReads, Google+ and various other social media sites can be very helpful. I'm not going to go over each one in detail, but some experimentation will help you find the ones you're comfortable with. The worst thing you can do is create accounts on these sites and act like a used car salesman. Add people that have the same interests as you, read their books, promote their interesting blog posts, maintain your own blog, be a *real* person—not just a person trying to sell a book.

Blogging can be an important part of building your platform as well. If you have interesting things to say about your process or topic, you can draw people to your site. Think of it as a writing sample. However, a word of caution about blogging—it should never take away from your *real* writing. You should never use a blog update as an excuse to miss a daily goal. I've seen too many people fall into this trap, and I feel I have to caution new indie writers. By all means, write interesting blog posts and bring readers to you, but make sure you continue to write while you do so.

Book Release

When you have established a platform, worked through editing, found a cover design you like and decided on a title (always the last thing for me), you should read your book one more time. Once you've done that, it's time to set a release date and make the final choices about your book.

Formats

You can publish your book in two different formats: print and eBooks. Regardless of whether you use them yourself, you can't ignore eBooks. I think that authors have more credibility when they offer both print and e-reader formats, at least for the Nook and Kindle, because it shows they understand the current publishing market. If you choose to do one or the other exclusively, you're alienating potential sales to the people who are firmly in one camp.

When I released *Inked,* I did not offer an eBook. I heard hundreds of times "Oh, that's too bad, I'd buy a copy on my Kindle" It *was* too bad—for me. I now offer all formats, and I see more eBook sales than physical copies.

Barnes and Noble's *Pub IT!* is an easy-to-use, direct to Nook, resource. Amazon has desktop publishing (DTP) as well for the Kindle format. Smashwords.com is a great resource for indie authors. Read up on these formats and learn how to adjust your layout for eBooks. It's not that hard and a few Google searches will help you learn the nuances.

Price Point

I think that the biggest mistake indie authors can make is over-pricing print books and underpricing eBooks. I know there have been "amazing but true" stories of success with $0.99 Kindle books, but when I see a $0.99 eBook I assume that it isn't good enough to sell at a higher price. While this may not be true, you should be aware that it gives a certain impression.

On the other hand, I don't want to spend $16.99 (plus $3-5 in shipping) on an indie book when I'm already taking a risk buying it in the first place. Yes, Dean Koontz can charge that much, but you don't have his audience.

When determining your print-price, decide what the minimum you'd like to make each book after all the costs of production (printing, shipping, etc.) and price it a dollar or two higher. This will allow you to run sales and specials in the future—especially in person. I sell my books for $10 in person, and people love deals. Your eBooks should be priced slightly lower than your print book, so once you know where you're comfortable pricing your print book (for me it's $13.99), lower that price by a couple dollars (I like $7.99) for the eBook.

Pre-Orders

Use the platform you've been building to create a buzz about your upcoming release. Set a reasonable date and announce special presale pricing. Oh, and autographs! I never in a million years thought that people would care about my autograph, but I was wrong. People love the personal connection of a signed book. Set up a reading or book-signing with local book stores, writers groups or other associations. These pre-sales will help you build up a little money to spend on advertising.

This is also the time to start offering free advance-reader copies. Send them out to good reviewers that you trust, asking for their feedback and online reviews. This will get people excited about your book.

Release Day!

Enjoy the release date of your book! Have a party with friends, relax with a glass of wine or schedule a reading at your favorite coffee shop. This is a big step, you deserve a moment in the spotlight. Take it and enjoy it. From here on out you're an author!

Talking About Your Book

You are your book's only salesman. You need to learn to talk about and sum it up in a way that is appealing to the people around you. Just like pitching to an agent, you only have a few seconds to grab them before you will lose their attention. It's important to feel out your listeners as well, don't drive them away because you are rambling on and on about your novel. Talk confidently about your art, let them know why they should read it but remain conscious of their time. They will remember you for your politeness.

You are now the author of *Insert Your Title Here,* and the moment you stop talking about your book is the moment it will stop selling. Be positive, talk about your writing and publishing experiences and people will want to listen.

One Sentence Pitch: _____

_____

Three Sentence Pitch: _____

_____

_____

My Genre: _____

My Comparable Books: _____

_____

My Target Audience: _____

After the Release

You're not going to be a millionaire or a guest on the *Today* show (quite yet), but you will feel a change in yourself. You're an AUTHOR now; you have a book! It's amazing. When someone asks what you do, you can answer with pride, "Let me tell you about my book!"

Once the book is out, you should continue to build and maintain your platform and presence, but you may also wonder, "What's next?" Writing, writing, and more writing. It's time to start thinking about plotting and planning your next book.

After all, you're an artist, right?

Renda Belle Dodge grew up in the Pacific Northwest as part of a typical, fractured family, and she currently resides in Seattle, Washington. Writing has always been a part of her life, and she began telling and illustrating stories when she was a child. Renda's writing style is bold and strives to capture the ongoing struggle for identity in contemporary America

She loves to read any interesting and quirky fiction. Her favorite authors are Plath, Cunningham, Chopin, Eugenides, Oates, Vonnegut and Bukowski. She loves listening to Amanda Palmer, Foo Fighters, The xx, Vanessa Carlton, Tegan and Sara, Alanis Morrisette and K's Choice. In her spare time, Renda spends a lot of time with her camera.

Renda is the Managing Editor of Pink Fish Press and _Line Zero_.

ThePinkFishPress.com
RendaDodge.com
LineZero.org

www.ingramcontent.com/pod-product-compliance
Lightning Source LLC
Chambersburg PA
CBHW080206300326
41934CB00038B/3388